Healthy Snacks To Go

Second Edition

Over 45 recipes to get you
on your way with real food, fast.
By Katie Kimball
KitchenStewardship.com

Table of Contents

Introduction

It's time to run out the door to practice/church/Grandma's house and you need to grab some snacks for the car, fast. You open up the cupboard and . . . all you see are ingredients.

It's a common problem for those of us who try to avoid processed foods. When you have to "process" everything yourself, eating away from home can be tricky. You can't pack ingredients! *Healthy Snacks To Go* to the rescue! With over 45 healthy snack recipes, including traditional granola bars, iron-packed Popeye bars, *plus* over a dozen "larabar" style variations, it is my hope that this book can reduce your travel stress and help your family eat more nourishing foods, no matter where you are.

Why Healthy Snacks?

When you're out and about, it's so tempting to run through fast food or buy something packaged that has less-than-ideal ingredients and often costs more than what you could make at home. You need simple, nourishing snacks that can handle being packed in a lunch or even hanging out in a diaper bag or desk drawer for days (weeks?). No one wants their food budget jacked up because of processed snacks, healthy or otherwise. Even at home, you need to be able to have something ready quickly to prevent hungry children from melting down at snack time.

Three Tips to Trick your Tongue

Sugar tastes great. It's also addicting. We all should try to cut down on the sugar or use an alternative, natural sweetener whenever possible. The ultimate goal is to cut out the sweeteners entirely, but that's a tough one!

You can cut down and still be kind to your sweet tooth by increasing three foods in your recipes that help make you think you're eating sweeter dishes than in reality:

1. Cinnamon
2. Vanilla
3. Coconut Oil

It's easy to add a teaspoon or more of cinnamon to waffles, pancakes, quick breads, and even some cookies while cutting down on or cutting out the sweetener. You can put vanilla in your plain yogurt or add some to power bars (date and nut bars) as seen on page 25.

Virgin coconut oil, the kind with full coconut flavor and aroma, is a good substitute for sugar in your morning oatmeal (I add cinnamon, too) or coffee, tastes great in smoothies (see p. 80), and is the star "hint of sweetness" in Take-Along Spelt Biscuits (p. 53) and Soaked Coconut Granola (p. 12).

Katie's Kitchen Supplies for From-Scratch Cooks

I avoid aluminum and non-stick surfaces when I can because of possible health hazards. I loooooove baking with my baking stone, which I purchased through Pampered Chef. For ease of mind *and* clean-up, I choose to line my old cookie sheets with a silicone baking mat, like, although I've since learned more about silicone's potential dangers. If you don't have either of those, for things like crackers (p. 46), you'll want some parchment paper.

Many *Healthy Snacks To Go* recipes benefit greatly from a food processor but are possible with a blender (preferably glass). I think both are worthwhile investments, or get one machine that does both. You'll want some muffin tins and a selection of glass baking dishes (I love that mine have lids) for optimal snack production, too.

We send a lot of snacks to school and keep trail mix in my purse with our reusable bags. That said, most of the recipes can be made with *no* special supplies or talent. Believe me, you don't need much talent to be a healthy cook, just motivation and commitment!

Yes, You Can Plan Snacks

If you're not a meal planner at all, you're going to struggle with real food preparation. Hopefully you already have a system in place – my challenge for you (and for myself!) is to start to add some snack plans in there.

I don't necessarily mean to plan out your snacks day-to-day, but to plan an opportunity once or twice a week to prepare some snacks.

Make crackers. Whip up some power bars. Boil some eggs. When the snacks are already prepared, you are ready to run out the door!

Ingredients Notes

Some ingredients from my real food kitchen might be new visitors in your kitchen, and that's okay. Be bold! Try something new. Here's a little cheat sheet to help you figure out what's going on:

- **Butter**: I don't get too picky about brands and origins, but mostly I use unsalted butter, and never, EVER the fake stuff.
- **Coconut oil**: "Refined" coconut oil is more processed and has no odor or flavor, while "unrefined" has both the smell and taste of coconuts. Some recipes call for one or the other for a reason, but many recipes could use either. Be sure to find well-processed coconut oil, pressed at low temps and mechanically, not chemically, extracted. Both forms of the oil are solid below 76F and liquid above.
- **Unsweetened coconut**: I never use sweetened coconut in any of my baking. That's what you generally find at a grocery store, but the sugar and random filler ingredients are atrocious, and besides that, the sweetened stuff doesn't even taste like real coconut. My whole life, I thought I didn't like coconut, until I tried unsweetened

coconut and unrefined coconut oil. Now I absolutely adore the flavor. Find unsweetened shredded coconut at a health foods store or online in bulk. (A list of resources is available here: http://bit.ly/ZFeIvb)

- **Flour options:**
  - All recipes should work with both freshly ground or storebought flours.
  - *Whole wheat flour* – traditional "hard red" wheat (the norm in a grocery store)
  - *White whole wheat* – "hard white" wheat if grinding your own; white whole wheat has no fewer nutrients than traditional whole wheat. It's simply a different strain of wheat plant, not anything about the way it's processed. King Arthur is a great brand to purchase.
  - *Whole wheat pastry flour* – from "soft white wheat" berries; this flour is good for cakes, muffins, biscuits and crackers, but terrible for breads or cookies.
  - *Spelt flour* – an older cousin of wheat, spelt does contain gluten, although less than traditional wheat. Spelt often lends a hint of sweetness to a recipe.

- **Sweeteners:** Read more about sucanat/rapadura, raw honey, and real maple syrup at KitchenStewardship.com – including links to scientific sources and studies.
  - **Unrefined Dehydrated Whole Cane Sugar** *(Sucanat, Rapadura, Panela and Muscovado):* Four names for the same thing.
    - Can be substituted 1:1 for white sugar but the molasses content will usually affect the taste of the recipe.
  - **Raw Honey:** Honey is one of the oldest sweeteners humans have been consuming, takes the least processing in my opinion, since the bees do almost all the work, and was also responsible for the first alcoholic mead . Honey, especially raw honey, also has some genuine nutritional health benefits: Anti-Bacterial, Anti-Viral, Anti-Fungal.
    - You can substitute honey for sugar in most baking recipes, but be sure to take the following steps:
      - Use 1/2 – 3/4 cup of honey for each one cup of sugar in the recipe.
      - Reduce the liquid by 1/4 cup for each cup of sugar replaced.
      - Reduce cooking temp by 25 degrees (honey will make your baked goods brown more easily).
      - If the recipe doesn't already include baking soda, add 1/4 tsp for each cup of sugar replaced.
  - **Maple syrup:** May be the healthiest sweetener yet. The catch is that it's often twice as expensive, so it's a big judgment call. Maple syrup has all sorts of health benefits not limited to antioxidant defense, 100% daily value of manganese in 1/4 cup, improves HDL cholesterol, is high in zinc for heart health and immune support and anti-inflammatory properties.
  - *If you're working on a budget, simply cut down on the sugars your family eats, period, and you'll spend less in the long run for better nutrition.*

- **Unrefined salt:**
  - Harvested sea salt that is not refined has over 60 different minerals in it (instead of the TWO found in regular table salt).
  - Unrefined salt will usually be colorful, with shades of pink, brown, or grey, depending on the source.
  - Some brands that help you make sure you're getting real, unrefined sea salt include Real Salt, Celtic Sea Salt, and Himalayan Salt.
  - Real, unrefined sea salt is a natural source of iodine. You can get the iodine your body needs from unrefined salt plus a balanced diet including "real" whole foods such as eggs, seaweed (I add this to my chicken stock), yogurt, strawberries and mozzarella cheese.
  - *The bottom line is that real, unrefined sea salt provides a natural balance of minerals that keeps us healthy instead of making us sick.*

What if I Don't Like Coconut?

Some folks have pointed out to me that a lot of these recipes call for shredded coconut or coconut oil. If you're allergic to coconuts or don't like it, you can fiddle with the recipes:

- Use refined coconut oil for some options like muffins, or just melted butter.
- Coconut *flour* doesn't taste like coconut; don't worry. If you want to dabble in grain-free or even gluten-free living, a bag goes a long way. It's my first recommended GF flour purchase. You can find links to my favorite brands on KitchenStewardship.com under "What to Buy: KS Recommends" or the special *Healthy Snacks to Go* resource page at http://bit.ly/ZFeIvb.
- Just leave the shredded coconut out in granola recipes, or sub in flax, chia seeds, or extra nuts/seeds.
- For most power bars, like Sunny Vacation or Mediterranean, you can just leave it out completely or try subbing in equivalent flax meal or sesame seeds just for bulk. Coco-shew is the only version that absolutely needs the coconut to survive.
- Sub in ground flax, chia seeds, sesame seeds, or skip in popeye and protein bars.
- For peanut butter kisses, try ground flax meal instead of coconut.

Exclusive Free Resources Available Online

Check out www.KitchenStewardship.com for more great ideas, recipes and tips. As the owner of the print edition of *Healthy Snacks to Go*, you also have access to extended resources and coupons at: http://bit.ly/ZFeIvb (including the opportunity for the PDF edition for only $2 so you can have your new favorite recipes on a mobile device or searchable on your home computer).

Features of the Text

Use these simple icons to figure out how difficult a recipe is, special allergy or dietary ingredients, cost, storage, and "how sweet it is!" There is also an ingredients key on the last page for easy reference.

 Sugar Free

 Gluten Free

 Casein (Dairy) Free

No Added Sweetener

 Grain Free

 Nut Free

 Raw Food (live enzymes)

S Soaked Option

¢ Frugal snack

$ Pricey but still less than processed

Diaper bag/backpack friendly

Some refrigeration needed

Work Intensity:

I don't tell you how much time a recipe will take. It really depends if you have to run to another area of the house for an ingredient or balance a fussy toddler or serve the kiddos an afternoon snack in the midst of your efforts. I'll just tell you the level of difficulty compared to something you might have already done, like baking cookies.

Easy: *As easy as slicing packaged cookies and baking them.*

Medium: *About as much work as baking cookies from scratch.*

Hard: *A lot of work, more like making cut-out sugar cookies and frosting from scratch.*

With each recipe, you'll also find:

   Timesaver Tips

⭐ Added Bonus Facts

Healthy Upgrades

May include less sugar options, soaked versions, or alternative sweeteners.

Basic Snacks for the Absent-Minded Eater

Every time someone mentions hard boiled eggs as a good snack, I smack my forehead and say, "Oh, yeah! I always forget about those!" It would be an easy thing to put in my calendar weekly to boil some eggs, but by the time snacktime rolls around, it's already too late.

Here's a list of forehead smackers to help you out when meal planning.

If you have a regular time or place or a regular printed system for planning your meals, you may want to copy this page to keep there as well. You can remind yourself of easy, healthy snacks by planning them into your week.

- ✔ Whole fruit, apples with peanut butter
- ✔ Dried fruit (see more about how to dry your own on p. 64)
- ✔ Veggies and dip (p. 70)
- ✔ Guacamole (dip veggies or tortilla chips)
- ✔ Nuts or crispy nuts
- ✔ Deviled eggs
- ✔ Popcorn (p. 51)
- ✔ Frozen peas – great finger food for toddlers and preschoolers
- ✔ Hard-boiled eggs
- ✔ Olives
- ✔ Cheese sticks, cheese and crackers
- ✔ Yogurt (ideas to spice it up on p. 80)
- ✔ PB&J, PB& Honey, or cream cheese and honey/jam sandwiches can be snacks, too!
- ✔ Toast, grilled cheese or pizza sauce and cheese on bread
- ✔ Trail mixes – if you see it in a store, you can bet you can mix it at home for less money.
- ✔ _____
- ✔ _____
- ✔ _____

 Timesaver: Slice a whole block of cheese, hard boil eggs, and cut vegetables once a week, and store them all in the fridge so there's a snack ready when you are.

More Ideas online http://bit.ly/ZFelvb

Katie's Homemade Granola

Work Intensity

Storage

Cost

I can still vividly remember taking my mom's homemade granola to school to eat as a snack on the playground. With just a touch of sweetness and refreshingly simple ingredients, her granola is a sure winner every time.

Ingredients

SF GF CF **S**

3 c. oats	¼ c. melted butter or coconut oil
½ c. sunflower seeds	¼ c. honey
½ c. chopped nuts	1/6 c. water (2 ½ Tbs.) optional: 1 tsp. cinnamon
½ c. coconut	1 tsp. vanilla

Method

Preheat oven to 350 degrees F. Mix (4) dry ingredients together in a large bowl. Mix (4) wet ingredients in a separate bowl.

Pour the wet mixture into the dry and stir well. (Add optional spice whenever – even after spreading on the pan.)

Transfer into a 9"x13" dish or rimmed cookie sheet, ungreased. Toast in the oven and stir after 10 minutes, then more frequently until browned (every 5-7 minutes). *See the low-temp baking option for forgetful people in the FAQs...*

Stir from the outside in and the bottom up. The granola will brown up a bit after you're finished, so stop just short of what you want it to look like. Allow to cool before storing in an airtight container.

Serve with milk like conventional cereal or as a to-go snack in a cup that kids can "drink," either with a milk next to it or just on its own. Tastes great with added cinnamon or dried fruit. Add dried fruit after the granola cools.

Makes about 10 half cup servings.

 Timesaver: Bake baked potatoes for dinner at the same time and save oven energy.

Healthy Upgrades:

 Soaked option: See the following recipe for the soaked option.

 Timesavers: Melt the oil in a pot big enough for dinner, and then use that pot for dinner!

Make applesauce rolls (p. 64) in the oven at the same time to save energy, or make a double batch of granola.

 Added Bonus: The time with the oven on is also a great chance to keep ferments like sourdough or kefir toasty warm sitting on the stovetop, or even to allow bread to rise.

 ## FAQs

- ✔ *What other spices have you tried?* I'm glad you asked. It's pretty fun to personalize your spices and experiment. My new favorite adds quite a feeling of fanciness in the morning: I add a ½ tsp. or so of cardamom. I'm sure pumpkin pie spice would be marvelous, and I bet you could even mix in some pureed pumpkin to the liquids before stirring into the oats (and likely even decrease the sweetener!). You can also change the flavor a lot with different nuts and dried fruit.
- ✔ *The granola isn't sticking together like commercial granola...is that right?* Yes, actually, each piece of oatmeal will remain individual. If you want clumpier, crunchy granola, check out the soaked coconut granola on the next page.
- ✔ *I keep burning the granola. Any tips?* I'm right there with you. Life is too distracting. I prefer now to bake at 200F for a couple hours, stirring every 45 minutes or so.
- ✔ *Can I use my dehydrator?* You bet! It takes about 12-15 hours to be crunchy (but I recommend just using the next recipe for good, crunchy granola).

Soaked Coconut Granola

Work Intensity

Storage

Cost

I never thought I'd like a granola better than my mom's, but the soft coconut flavor and the crunchy texture take this one clearly a step above. Double batch measurements included!

Ingredients

SF 🚫

3 c. rolled oats (6 c. for double batch)
¼ c. whole wheat flour (½ c.)
1 Tbs. whey + warm water to make 1 cup (2 Tbs. + 2 c.)
¼ c. + 2 Tbs. melted unrefined coconut oil (¾ c.)
¼ c. honey (½ c.)

1 tsp. vanilla (2 tsp.)
½ c. sunflower seeds (1 c.)
½ c. chopped nuts (1 c.)
½ c. coconut (1 c.)
1 tsp. cinnamon (2 tsp.)

Method

Combine oats and flour. Put whey or yogurt in a measuring cup and add water (warmed to about 120 degrees F is best) to make one cup. Mix into oats, stir well, and allow to rest at room temperature 12-24 hours. (If you want, you can add the oil and/or coconut now.)

When ready to bake, melt the coconut oil and stir together with the honey and vanilla in the pan. If you need any water to get things mixed and be pourable, add a few tablespoons. (If you added the coconut oil last night, just whisk honey with water and vanilla.)

Add cinnamon to soaked oats along with coconut, sunflower seeds, and nuts. (If using dehydrated crispy nuts and the oven to bake, wait until the end to combine.) You can use a pastry blender to help combine the ingredients if the soaked oats are very sticky.

In an oven: Spread onto a pan, cookie sheet, or baking stone as thinly as possible and toast in a 250 degree F oven for 2 ½-3 hours. Flipping the granola halfway through ensures crispy success. Turn oven off and leave granola inside (overnight is great) to finish drying.

Note: if you have an electric oven, it will continue producing heat after you turn it off. You need to stop baking a bit early and check every 20-30 minutes to make sure your granola is not burning.

For those trying to preserve the enzymes in a batch of crispy nuts, combine nuts or seeds along with granola before storing in an airtight container; refrigerate if sunflower seeds or crispy walnuts are used.

Tip: I have a jar of the nuts and seeds (sesame, too) kept cold and the nutless granola in the pantry to save on fridge/freezer space. This nut mixture also adds nourishment and flavor to hot oatmeal.

In a dehydrator: It couldn't be easier – just spread on parchment paper, mesh trays, or whatever will hold small pieces in your dehydrator, and dehydrate somewhere between 120-150F for 12-24 hours until crunchy. I have a new habit of making a triple batch of this and a double or triple of grain-free granola from the next page, filling the dehydrator right up for a day. I prefer the dehydrator because it's simply easier, but as long as you don't burn the granola in the oven, the "toasted" flavor of the oats is really quite nice.

Makes about 8 cups.

Timesaver: Just make a triple batch! It's fun!

Added Bonus: This soaked version is good finger food for little ones because there are clumps of granola perfect for nibbling on. It has also become one of the standbys I bring, along with homemade yogurt, for brunch potlucks.

 ## FAQs

- ✔ *Why add whole wheat flour?* See page 82 for a quick grain soaking primer.
- ✔ *Can I soak dairy-free?* Use lemon juice instead of whey and coconut oil for butter.
- ✔ *How about gluten-free?* The role of the wheat is phytase, which is also in buckwheat (gluten-free). Freshly ground is best.
- ✔ *Why not dehydrate at the lowest possible oven temp?* If your oven is like mine and doesn't go below 170F, you're killing everything anyway. You only need to go low enough so as to not scorch the granola. At 250F, you can start the cereal at dinner or afterward and still be awake to turn off the oven. Do keep an eye out for overbrowning, especially the first time you make the recipe. Burnt granola tastes so awful; I wouldn't wish it on anyone.
- ✔ *Is the soaked option just as tasty?* Yes, but different. It's less sweet, perhaps because the oats swell a bit when soaked and there isn't as much honey, ratio-wise. However, it's crunchy and more like boxed cereal now.
- ✔ *What if my soaked granola isn't crispy in the morning?* You can turn the oven back to 250F for 30-60 minutes, or if just a few chunks were too large or in the center of the pan and are a bit moist, just have your first bowl with those and make sure the crunchy pieces are the ones that get stored.

Cardamom Spiced Grain-free Granola

Work Intensity   Storage   Cost

Sometimes going on an elimination diet, like getting rid of gluten or grains, is really painful. This granola will renew your faith in a grain-free world. It might even taste better than my soaked granola, but don't go blabbing that too loudly.

Ingredients

- ¼ c. maple syrup
- ¼ c. honey or any other liquid sweetener (including up to half molasses)
- ¼ c. butter or unrefined coconut oil (or mixture of both)
- 1 ½ tsp. vanilla
- 2 c. almonds
- 2 c. other nut (walnuts, peanuts, cashews, pecans)
- 1 c. pumpkin or sunflower seeds
- 1 c. coconut
- 1/3 c. sesame seeds, optional
- 1 tsp. cinnamon
- ½ tsp. cardamom
- 1 c. dried fruit

Method

Over low to medium heat, melt the fat and sweeteners together until the mixture is completely liquid. Remove from heat and stir in vanilla. If you have liquified coconut oil (I keep mine in a glass jar on the stove), you could certainly retain the raw properties of the honey by simply mixing together at room temperature.

Food process briefly or chop almonds so that they're the size you want, which can be quite small but not finely ground. Do the same to the second type of nut, keeping some larger chunks if you like.

Mix nuts with seeds, coconut and spices. Pour the liquid mixture over the top and stir well.

Spread granola in a thin layer on a large cookie sheet. (You could add the spices at this point, sprinkling on top, especially if you'd like to try some with and some without.) Removal for storage is easiest if you have a silicone mat liner or parchment paper, but be sure to reuse the paper as much as possible.

Stir in dried fruit after toasting.

In an oven: Bake in a preheated oven at 350F for 15-20 minutes, stirring after the first 8 minutes and every 3-5 after that. Watch edges for over-browning. Cool partway and package in airtight containers while still slightly warm. The granola will crisp up and stick together more and more while it cools. If you let it cool completely, you just might have the biggest granola bar you've ever seen.

In a dehydrator: Spread evenly on dehydrator sheets, using fine mesh, flat plastic or parchment paper to prevent the shredded coconut, sesame seeds, etc. from falling through. Dehydrate at anywhere from 110-145F (you could combine with something else) until fairly dry, usually about 12-24 hours.

I prefer the dehydrator for 4 reasons: (1) I don't have to stir or monitor (2) I can't over-brown the granola, no matter how long I forget about it, and (3) I think it tastes better gently dried than toasted, and (4) my raw honey and crispy nuts retain enzymes.

Storage: If you use crispy walnuts or seeds, technically storage should be cold. If you have room in the fridge, do that. If not, room temperature storage should be fine for a few weeks.

Serve with milk like a cold cereal or in a "to go" cup dry.

Makes about 8 cups.

 Timesaver: I love to make a triple batch of soaked granola (p. 12) and a double batch of this recipe in the dehydrator at the same time.

 Added Bonus: You can start your day with a quick, protein-packed meal to get you going.

Healthy Upgrades or Variations

Soaked option: For optimal nourishment, follow the directions for crispy nuts first (http://bit.ly/ZFeIvb).

Less crunchy variation: For some, all these nuts are just too crunchy and dense. One reader used the 5 total cups nuts and seeds and then 5 cups of coconut flakes (not shredded coconut) instead of just one. The flakes have a great texture after baking.

Adapted from Heartland Renaissance.

Snack Bar Manifesto

After I published the first edition of *Healthy Snacks to Go*, I remained amazed at the popularity of *bars*. **People just love snack bars**. The original granola bars at Kitchen Stewardship have consistently been the most popular recipe on the site, and people are constantly telling me, "We just love your granola bars; we make them all the time."

While homemade yogurt might be great for my family to snack on when we're home, the reality is that when people need snacks in our fast-paced culture, they're almost always on the go. **A bar delivers it all: a single serving, easy to hold, easy to serve children, easy to eat wherever you are.** It's no wonder this little book has 7 kinds of bars with a total of 21+ variations, a whopping 45% of the total number of recipes!

Everyone loves something different, too. There are the crunchy bar aficionados, the sticky sweet tooth types, and the give-me-as-many-food-groups-as-you-can-fit-in-a-bar nutrition nuts.

I've had a love-hate relationship with my own granola bar recipe since I posted it almost three years ago. At first, I was just excited to graduate from my previous recipe, which used puffed cereal, something I was trying to stay away from. When the recipe took off as a favorite at KS, it was fun to just go with the flow and keep up the excitement some more. I loved experimenting with soaked oats and the "no-bake" version. And then I published the book, still excited to share all this with the world.

Once that was off to the virtual presses, **I continued making both granola bar recipes** because my family, like many others, just loved them.

On my first "soaked" batch after the release of Healthy Snacks to Go, I created an utter fail. The bars wouldn't stick together unless I squeezed a chunk in my hand into a ball, and still, I'm pretty sure as many crumbs got on the floor than into my then 2-year-old.

Um.

What have I done? I can't even follow my own recipe? (This was before I utilized recipe testers for my books.) I actually had to get back on my computer to check the photographs. Yep, there was proof, in full color: **I had made the bars before, completely successfully. What was I doing wrong?**

I had similar problems, although slightly more firm than "granola," with the original baked recipe. Each batch seemed to degenerate further into crumb-dom than the last. I couldn't figure it out: why were thousands of people falling in love with a recipe that only sort of worked?

I've been working for the last two years to figure it out.

I'm thrilled to share the new and improved versions of both recipes, which have been tried and tested...and **they stay together**.

I've also added many style notes to the power bars now that I've been making them quite regularly for another year and a half, so they should be an easier task for even the novice cook.

What Bar to Choose?

If you're gazing at the table of contents in *Healthy Snacks to Go* and just don't know where to start, let me summarize the pros and cons of each "bar choice" you'll have:

Famous KS Granola Bars – oatmeal based and a close relative to a cookie bar, these are huge kid pleasers, your everyday granola bar. There is a gluten-free option.

No-Bake Granola Bars – more like the texture of a Quaker chewy bar, very sweet, includes a soaked option, and if it's hot and you don't want to turn the oven on, this is your winner. However – they stay together best with a re-toast in the oven. Naturally gluten-free (with GF oats).

Power Bars – made of dried fruit and nuts (like a Larabar). I prefer making balls because they're easy to carry and a great size for little ones. No grains, no sugar, but lots of sweetness from the dried fruit. Great for summer because there's no baking involved and they last forever in the backpack, but you do need a food processor or blender.

Popeye Bars – grain-free and iron-fortified with molasses. A perfect choice for the most nutrient-conscious, but not always kid-friendly. Must bake or dehydrate.

Protein Bars – the less expensive, more kid-friendly brother of Popeye Bars. Still grain-free but with peanut butter included; these also seem to last forever.

Almond Power Bars – the "grown-up" of the crowd. These bars seem more refined, like you could serve them as a fancy appetizer (or dessert!). However, they do need to be refrigerated to really stay together, so they're not as travel-worthy as many others. No baking, but a food processor is necessary.

Butternut Spice Bars – If you need more vegetables in your diet, this is the way to do it. These guys are grain-free and super easy to make, but do require both baking and refrigeration, so they can't be an emergency car snack (but make a great source of protein, fats, and vitamins for the 10 a.m. break at school).

The Perfection of a Granola Bar

Even though thousands love the KS granola bars, they had that annoying crumbly problem and used a whole cup of honey, which I hoped to cut down.

I tried adding an egg.
I tried reducing the honey and using applesauce instead, just to reduce the sweetener. Eh.
I tried fewer oats.
I tried various baking time and temperature changes, but nothing seemed to help quite *enough*.

I read about adding pureed dates, but getting out the food processor takes these from basic to complicated, and it was important to me to try hard to keep this a simple, everyday recipe.

Carrying on...

I tried less butter (that helps a bit).
I tried less flour.

I cut the flour entirely (that, by the way, makes granola. Nothing sticks together at all, which led me to...)

I could not believe what finally worked: more flour. It flew in the face of reason, because I always thought flour would make a baked good dry and crumbly. Not so. Adding a half cup of flour made the bars have more stick-together-ness than ever before.

For the no-bake bars, I just needed to make sure that the sweetener/fat mixture cooked to a high enough temperature that it reaches the "soft ball" stage, but I didn't want folks to have to bust out a thermometer just to make granola bars. A handful of happy testers assure me I've done it!

And finally, thanks to a brilliant commenter at the original granola bar post from 2009, I learned this trick, which seals the deal on perfecting both versions:

The stick together trick

Toast any granola bar or the protein/Popeye bars from this book to help them stay together better: Just spread individual bars out on a baking sheet or stone, using parchment paper or a silicone mat if you choose, and bake at 350-ish for 5-15 minutes, depending on the bar. Toss them in after you've baked dinner to save energy (which is where that "ish" comes into play – 325-375F is a good range for the great bar toast).

Reports from my testers...

"I just tried the updated version of your granola bar recipe. I have been making your granola bars for quite some time now and we have always loved them. I love the updated version for toasting them in the oven. The crunch on the outside with the soft inside is delicious. Now I have to go toast the other half of the bars. I thought I would try some toasted and some not toasted, but I have to say that I am a fan of the toasted.

I just wanted to let you know that the granola bars are holding up and keeping their shape really well. I can break them in half and I don't get any crumbs that break off. Also, when my son brings his lunch box home for me to empty out his garbage, I have noticed very little crumbs from the granola bars in his bag. Less crumbs on the floor, too, when my little one is walking around the kitchen eating her granola bar. All in all I think that adding that extra 1/2 cup of flour and toasting them in the oven really did make a huge difference in the crumbliness."   --T

"I cut one for each of my boys and gave them to them for an after school snack. I told them I needed to know what they thought of them because I was testing the recipe for a friend and they said, "YES YES YES!! We love them! Can we have them every day for a snack?!?" So I think they're a hit!

I cannot believe I have not made your granola bars yet! I have another recipe that I have been using, but they are crumbly and take more time...These were easy as anything to mix up! I'm a convert. "   --H

"I did the "crispier" option. I was very skeptical when they came out of the oven...they looked much less together than after they came out of the fridge...I was thinking I shouldn't have tried that part. But after they cooled they were perfect! Just like a Quaker bar in consistency! We even tested them out on a local zoo trip, and they passed the test on the go too!"
          --N

Honestly, I'm going to keep fiddling with them just to have more options than ever. My next three tests will be cutting the baking soda, adding a Tbs. flax meal mixed with 2 Tbs. water, and cutting the butter in half. We won't be hurting for snacks in the Kimball house!

 Star Qualities

Best for backpacking...power bars or Popeye/protein bars

Best for school lunch...granola bars, re-toasted...or any other recipe in this book! Ha!

Best for emergency car snacks...KS granola bars or power bars

Best to serve others...almond power bars

Best for stick-to-your-ribs staying power... Popeye, protein, or almond power bars

Best for quick energy...power bars

Best for nutrients...butternut spice bars or Popeye bars (although many others close behind)

Best for budget...KS granola bars, no-bake bars or butternut spice bars

Kitchen Stewardship Granola Bars

Work Intensity

Storage

Cost

The most popular recipe at Kitchen Stewardship, this granola bar method is as easy as mixing up a batch of homemade cookies. The amount of honey makes them both slightly indulgent and slightly expensive, but it's worth it!

Ingredients

1 c. butter, softened

1 c. honey

1 tsp. vanilla

4 1/2 c. rolled oats

1 ½ c. whole wheat or spelt flour

1 tsp. baking soda

2 cups of add-ins: mini semi-sweet chocolate chips, chopped walnuts, dried fruit, sunflower seeds, coconut, other nuts…

Makes at least 20 bars, equivalent to about 3 boxes processed bars

Method

Lightly butter a 9"×13" glass pan. In a large mixing bowl, cream butter, honey, and vanilla. **Tip**: *If your butter isn't softened, use a rolling pin and roll it between two sheets of wax paper. Or mash it with your hands while in the wrapper. Our secret.*

Add the oats, flour, and baking soda. Beat well until combined. Stir in add-ins by hand. Press mixture hard into pan. (You can use your hands!)

Bake at 325 degrees F for 15-22 minutes until just golden brown on the edges. You will think they are too soft. They are not. Just remind yourself that there's not even any egg in the recipe, so you can't hurt anybody if you underbake. Allow to cool for at least 10 minutes before cutting into bars. Let bars cool completely in pan before removing and serving. Store at room temperature or freeze.

Stickier, Chewier Granola Bars: The one drawback of this original recipe is that it tends to be a bit crumbly, especially if you overbake the bars even slightly. You can avoid that by melting the butter, honey and vanilla in a saucepan and cooking on low for 5 minutes after the butter melts, then mixing the liquid ingredients into the dry.

Crispy Bars *(the stick together trick):* After cooling and cutting bars apart, place them separately on a cookie sheet or baking stone, spaced out at least an inch from one another. Toast in a 325-350F oven for 10-13 minutes until just browning on the edges. Watch closely for over-browning. You will think this trick didn't work when you take them out, but don't touch! Let everything cool completely right on the cookie sheet, and you'll have a healthy snack that truly deserves the term "to go." Once *completely cooled*, they will be slightly crispy on the outside and have much more structural integrity.

A reader also tells me one can take parchment paper and simply manually press down on the just-baked bars, compressing them, which holds them together well.

Variations

✔ Add ¼ c. cocoa powder to the dry ingredients; no chocolate chips needed.
✔ Use ½ c. natural peanut butter, almond butter or sunbutter in place of ½ c. of the butter (stay on the short side of baking time as nut butters can dry out the bars).
✔ Use a large cookie sheet and press the bars more thinly, then do the 'crispy bar' trick for totally crispy granola bars (or put a half batch into a 9x13 pan – just be sure to really press them together before baking).

 Timesaver: Make at the same time as Katie's Homemade Granola (p. 10) – many of the ingredients are the same, and if you bake the granola first, it's even possible to use the same 9"x13" glass pan.

Healthy Upgrades

 See the no-bake version on the next page for a few different ways to make these bars with soaked and dehydrated oats. You can also use crispy nuts for easier digestibility.

FAQs

✔ *Can I make these gluten free?* Just sub GF all-purpose flour for the whole wheat and it should work fine, according to a reader. Another used a cup mixed sorghum and brown rice flour plus a teaspoon of xanthan gum.
✔ *How about dairy free?* Coconut oil works fine in place of butter.
✔ *How long is the shelf life?* Seriously, I found a bar in our diaper bag that had been there for months, and it was perhaps a bit lower on the quality scale, but no mold or other issues that would deem them inedible. Generally they are gone so quickly you don't have to worry about shelf life!
✔ *Can I use less honey?* Honey is expensive and the "unhealthy" ingredient in this recipe. When you heat the honey, you can definitely cut it down by at least 1/3 cup and everything still holds together. I also had success substituting natural applesauce for up to 1/2 cup honey, but the resulting bars weren't very sweet. The chocolate chips were a necessity.
✔ *Do I need raw honey?* No. In fact, you'll lose any health benefits of the raw honey by baking the bars, so you may want to use the least expensive honey you can find.

I am indebted to Faith and Family Magazine for the original recipe and to Donielle at Naturally Knocked Up for her soaked granola bar recipe, which inspired the no-bake version and are also delicious!

No-Bake Granola Bars

Work Intensity   Storage   Cost

A gluten-free, soaked version of the famous KS granola bars? Yes, exactly. Although the ingredients are nearly the same, the taste is so very different because of the preparation. I think these guys are even closer to the ol' Quaker processed stuff!

Ingredients

 SF

½ c. sucanat
½ c. honey
¾ c. butter
1 tsp. vanilla
4 c. rolled oats or soaked and dried oats
1 c. chopped nuts + 1 c. add-ins (see Variations)

Method

Cook the sucanat, honey and butter in a small pot over low to medium-low heat until slowly bubbling, stirring often. Leave on the heat for at least 10 minutes after boil.

In a large bowl, mix the oats, nuts, and any add-ins (leave chocolate chips out until the end to avoid melting them).

When the liquid is finished on the stove, remove from heat and add vanilla (and peanut butter, if using – see variations). Stir until melty and thoroughly combined.

Pour syrup over oat mixture and stir until uniform. If using chocolate chips, add them afterward once things have cooled slightly.

Press into a 9x13 pan (or any container, really, even plastic) lined with wax paper. Freeze 30 minutes (or refrigerate a few hours) and cut into bars. Can store at room temperature, but hold together *best* when cold.

Makes about 2 dozen bars, depending on how you slice them.

Variations

Add-in ideas:
- o mini chocolate chips
- o chopped nuts
- o dried fruit
- o shredded coconut
- o ground flax seed (but I wouldn't recommend a whole cup)
- o sunflower or pumpkin seeds
- o 1 tsp. cinnamon or other favorite spices

Peanut Butter: Use ½ c. creamy natural peanut butter and ¼ c. butter in place of the ¾ c. butter.

Less sweetener: I haven't tried it, but I bet you could cut the sucanat in half and still have workable bars. Because the sugars are holding everything together, just be ready to create granola instead of granola bars, just in case! :)

Alternative sweeteners: Brown sugar is an acceptable (but not as healthy) substitute for sucanat, and maple syrup should work in place of honey but will change the flavor.

If you'd like to *avoid all granulated sweeteners*, use a whole cup of honey, no sucanat, and follow the directions as written, but if you want to store them at room temperature, you may have more trouble with them holding together. However – follow the "crispy" directions below with honey-only bars, and you're back in business.

Crispier bars: After refrigerating or freezing, cut bars apart then spread individually on a baking sheet or stone and toast again for ~10-13 minutes in a preheated 325-350F oven. Watch closely for overbrowning. You will think this trick didn't work when you take them out, but *don't touch! Trust me on this one.* I promise they're not the pile of mush they look like they have become. Let everything cool completely right on the cookie sheet, and you will have sturdy, crunchy granola bars to die for.

 Soaked option*:* Use soaked and dehydrated oats in this recipe with great success.

 Timesaver: Bake granola just before and reuse the same bowl and pot.

 # FAQs

- ✓ *How do I make this dairy free?* Use coconut oil in place of the butter.

- ✓ *Can I use crunchy peanut butter?* Why not? One of the testers loved it!

- ✓ *These are hard to cut apart!* If you use the freezer method especially, you may struggle to cut the bars. Either use a sharp knife or consider scoring them before freezing.

- ✓ *Fridge or backpack? What gives?* Don't be intimidated by the fact that these bars go in the fridge for a smidge. They are *definitely* backpack friendly. If you find one that has fallen apart, you can honestly smash it together in your fist and get a big old granola ball. Tasty! Also, try the toasting method for crispier bars. They really are still quite soft and chewy, just with more stick-together-ness than before.

- ✓ *Can I toast the oats first?* Toasting the oats beforehand adds another layer of flavor to the bars (and makes them look prettier).

Power Bars *(reverse engineered Larabars)*

Work Intensity   **Storage**   **Cost**

I can't justify spending over $1 each on brand name fruit and nut bars when it's so easy to make them at home. Here are 15 varieties of nutrient dense, enzyme rich bars that are easy to pack, easy to eat, and fairly painless to put together.

Some are reverse engineered from actual packages, other are simply inspired by what was in my pantry. Be sure to study the basic method and FAQs <u>first</u>, and you'll be well equipped to start experimenting. Then enjoy some family taste tests to discover your favorite flavors!

Method

Use the same basic steps every time:
1. In a food processor, **pulse or process nuts** until chopped finely, a "meal" consistency at the smallest. Be sure not to end up with nut butter by accident!
2. **Add dried fruit and process until everything is sticky** and there are no large chunks. (i.e., When the food processor stops jumping around, move on to step 3.)
3. Add any other mix-ins (like coconut) and pulse briefly until combined.
4. While the food processor is running, **stream in any spices, oil, or vanilla.**
5. If the mixture doesn't come together in a ball easily, **add water** while the food processor is running, ¼ tsp. at a time. When the mixture just starts to swish around in a blob instead of being crumbly, that's enough. I used to be worried about adding too much water and suggested "one drop at a time." Worry less. A little moisture won't hurt, and they really do stick together better. Just don't add a Tbs. at a time!
6. **Form the final product.** Either:
   a. Scrape mixture into any type of square of rectangular container and press firmly; cutting bar shapes is easier after refrigeration. You can line the dish with waxed paper for simpler removal, and I recommend using a piece of waxed paper to help you press everything as solidly packed as possible.
   b. Form individual bars with waxed paper, one at a time.
   c. Roll the mixture into balls, ½"-1" wide. *My favorite for easy serving to kids!*
7. Store in the refrigerator for best quality and firm bars, however, room temperature doesn't hurt any of these ingredients (unless you're using crispy walnuts or sunflower seeds, which should be refrigerated anyway).

Once you get the process down and understand the ratios of dried fruit to nuts, you can play around with new varieties on your own! I used this post as a jumping off point.
Makes 5-6 1 ½" x 3" bars or about a dozen ½-inch balls

FAQs

- *Why so many varieties?* First, with so many choices, you can start with what's already in your pantry and make something right away. Find the recipe that fits your stock. Then you can experiment with other varieties and find your favorites. We like them all, but some are better than others. In group taste tests, everyone had a favorite, but never the same bar. I'm convinced that each family will have different opinions, and there's certainly something for everyone here!

- *I don't have dates/I've never bought dates before. What do I do?* You can likely find dates near the raisins in your local grocery store. I bought them for the first time just for this, too! There are a few bars that don't call for dates at all. Also, any power bar will work with raisins in place of dates, but the flavor changes dramatically. I made the PBJ version with dates and with raisins, and one taste tester said, "This one (dates) tastes like peanut butter and jelly, but this one (raisins) has something else in it, right?" The raisins didn't make it taste *poorly*, but the other flavors had a hard time competing with the raisins.

- *Pitted or whole dates?* Depends on how much work you want to do! I'd vote that pitted is well worth the extra 30 cents/pound. Just not chopped; those include flour to prevent sticking, which we don't want in this recipe.

- *The mixture doesn't seem to stick together very well. What do I do?* Because of wide variation in the moisture level of different dried fruit, there's no way to provide the perfect ratio of fruit to nuts. If your bars aren't sticky enough, add ¼ teaspoon water or coconut oil at a time. You'll know you've added enough when the mixture inside the food processor starts to stick together while it's turning.

- *Can I use a blender instead of a food processor?* Yes. It's possible, but it's much more of a hassle. Blender tips:
  - Only make a single batch in a blender.
  - Start on very low speeds and move to higher speeds. Experiment with what your blender can handle.
  - Scrape the sides often.
  - Expect mixture to be not-so-sticky. I recommend balls instead of bars.
  - Unscrew the jar from the blade and extract your mixture from the bottom rather than trying to "pour" it out the top.

- *My machine is going to break!* Perhaps your dried fruit is too dry. I had some dates that were so hard, I had to soak them in water before I could use them.

- *Are power bars expensive or frugal?* Compared to potato chips, these are pricey items. Compared to name brand Larabars, however, you can almost make an entire batch for the cost of one bar. You'll get so many more nutrients from power bars than most processed snack food, so the question is about priorities.

- *How can I find good deals on these ingredients?* Watch the sales on basic dried fruit like apricots and raisins, and try buying dates in bulk from a health food store or co-op. Buy nuts on sale or in bulk and freeze until you need them.

- *Why aren't the batches bigger? This doesn't make enough for us!* My hope is that you'll try many versions the first few times, then make double batches of your favorites! I've also added a big batch conversion chart in the 2nd edition!

Ingredients

Basic Date and Nut Bars
Grind: 1/8 c. walnuts, ¼ c. almonds
Add: ½ c. dates, 1/8 c. raisins
Stream in: 1 Tbs. coconut + 4 tsp. cocoa powder + ½ Tbs. coconut oil + pinch instant coffee
optional: ½ tsp. mint extract (*this takes it from a plain old bar to something unique*)

Cherry Almond
Simply delightful; a crowd pleaser.
Grind: 1/3 c. almonds
Add: ¼ c. dates, 1/3 c. dried cherries
Stream in: scant ¼ tsp. ground cinnamon
If necessary, add water ¼ tsp. at a time to hold together.

German Chocolate
Don't tell people they're eating something healthy, and they'll never be the wiser.
Grind: ½ oz. unsweetened chocolate, 1/3 c. pecans, 1/4 c. almonds
Add: ½ c. dates
Stream in: 2 tsp. cocoa powder + ¼ c. shredded, unsweetened coconut
Add: 1 tsp. coconut oil until sticky

Mediterranean in the Tropics (No dates!)
The apricots set this version apart.
Grind: ¼ c. sunflower seeds, 1/3 c. almonds
Add: ¼ c. raisins, ¼ c. dried pineapple, ¼ c. dried apricots
Add: ¼ c. coconut
Stream in: ¼ tsp. vanilla + ¼ tsp. ground cinnamon

Sunny Vacation (Nut free!)
Sunflower seeds and apricots are the star players in this bar.
Grind: ¼ c. sunflower seeds
Add: ½ c. dates, ¼ c. dried apricots
Add: ¼ c. coconut
Stream in: ½ tsp. vanilla + 1/8 tsp. ground cinnamon
Add: ½-1 tsp. coconut oil until it holds together

Cinnamix (Cinnamon Trail Mix)
If you like cinnamon, this one's for you!
Grind: 1/3 c. almonds, ¼ c. cashews (also great with pecans or walnuts instead of cashews)
Add: ½ c. dates, ¼ c. raisins
Stream in: 1+ tsp. ground cinnamon

PBJ
An especially kid-friendly choice!
Grind: 1/3 c. peanuts
Add: ½ c. dates (can use raisins, but will change taste a lot), ¼ c. dried cherries
Stream in: <1/4 tsp. salt + optional ½ tsp. coconut oil (to hold together)

Tropical
You can almost smell the ocean air.
Grind: ¼ c. almonds, 1 Tbs. cashews
Add: ½ c. dates, 1/3 c. dried pineapple
Add: 1/3 c. coconut
Stream in: ½ tsp. dried orange peel + 1-2 tsp. coconut oil + ½ tsp. vanilla

Gingersnap
Spice! That's all you need to know.
Grind: 1/3 c. almonds, ¼ c. pecans
Add: ¾ c. dates
Stream in: ¼-½ tsp. ginger + ¼ tsp. cinnamon + ¼ tsp. cloves

Coco-shew *(Date free!)*
My personal favorite; sweet and salty.
Grind: 1/3 c. cashews
Add: ½ c. raisins, ¼ c. coconut
Stream in: ½ tsp. vanilla

Peanutty Bars
Simplicity at its best.
Grind: ¼ c. peanuts
Add: ½ c. dates
Stream in: slightly less than ¼ tsp. Salt

Chocolate Peanut Butter Delight
It's almost a Reese's, but without the sugar. Be careful not to overprocess.
Grind: 1/3 c. peanuts, 2-3 Tbs. chocolate chips or dark chocolate
Add: ½ c. dates
Stream in: ½ tsp. vanilla

Zesty Cranberry
Any variety of nuts would fit the bill with dried cranberries.
Grind: 1/3 c. pecans (pulse gently)
Add: ½ c. dates, 1/3 c. dried cranberries
Stream in: generous ¼ tsp. vanilla + 1/8-1/4 tsp. cinnamon + ¼ tsp. dried orange peel (optional)
squirt of honey (optional)

Bible Bars
Don't these ingredients smack of Old Testament and the Holy Land? You can call them something else if you like; this title cracks me up!
Grind: 1/3 c. walnuts
Add: ¼ c. dried figs, ½ c. dates
Stream in: squirt of honey

Apple Pie
Drying your own apples makes this one super frugal...and delicious.
Grind: 1/3 c. almonds, 1/3 c. walnuts
Add: ½ c. dates (can use some raisins), ½ c. dried apples
Stream in: 1/2+ tsp. cinnamon

Disclaimer: I am in no way affiliated with the Larabar company and am not applying the trademarked name to my bars.

Timesaver: Making double batches of one version and/or multiple kinds at once saves a lot of time in getting ingredients out and washing the food processor. You can even leave the food processor unwashed for a day or two while you find the time to make more. Not that I would do that...

 Added Bonus: It's like pre-chewed food! Particularly for toddlers who might not be able to handle whole nuts, or even older children who are notorious for eating too fast and not chewing, I feel like a power bar will give these expensive ingredients a better chance of being digested and absorbed.

Healthy Upgrades:

S If you want to reduce the anti-nutrients in the nuts, be sure to soak and dehydrate them. See directions for basic "crispy nuts" at the resources page: http://bit.ly/ZFelvb.

Skip a soaking step – you can measure and soak the nuts in water, drain them well and optionally pat dry, then simply use in the recipe without dehydrating. I recommend storing the finished bars in the refrigerator as much as possible with this method.

Some folks use these for energy during a long workout, like marathon training or 20-mile bike rides. You may want to add a bit of Real Salt to the mix for minerals and electrolytes as well.

Nut-free needed? Sunny Vacation is naturally nut-free, using only sunflower seeds. Try pepitas (pumpkin seeds) in some of those that are low on nuts like Zesty Cranberry, Bible Bars, even German Chocolate. Switch out almonds for more seeds in Mediterranean in the Tropics.

Big Batch Chart for Power Bars

	Grind:	Add:	Stream:
Basic Date and Nut Bars	1/8 c. walnuts, ¼ c. almonds	½ c. dates, 1/8 c. raisins	1 Tbs. coconut + 4 tsp. cocoa powder + ½ Tbs. coconut oil + pinch instant coffee
Double	¼ c. walnuts, ½ c. almonds	1 c. dates, ¼ c. raisins	2 Tbs. coconut + 3 Tbs. cocoa powder + ½ Tbs. coconut oil + pinch instant coffee
Quad	½ c. walnuts, 1 c. almonds	2 c. dates, ½ c. raisins	4 Tbs. coconut + 5 Tbs. cocoa powder + 1 Tbs. coconut oil + pinch instant coffee
Cherry Almond	1/3 c. almonds	¼ c. dates, 1/3 c. dried cherries	scant ¼ tsp. ground cinnamon
Double	2/3 c. almonds	½ c. dates, 2/3 c. cherries	½ tsp. cinnamon
Quad	1 1/3 c. almonds	1 c. dates, 1 1/3 c. cherries	1 tsp. cinnamon
If necessary, add water ¼ tsp. at a time to hold together.			
German Chocolate	½ oz. unsweetened chocolate, 1/3 c. pecans, 1/4 c. almonds	½ c. dates	2 tsp. cocoa powder + ¼ c. shredded, unsweetened coconut
Double	1 oz. chocolate, 2/3 c. pecans, ½ c. almonds	1 c. dates	1 Tbs. cocoa powder + ½ c. coconut
Quad	2 oz. chocolate, 1 1/3 c. pecans, 1 c. almonds	2 c. dates	2 Tbs. cocoa + 1 c. coconut
Add ½-1 tsp. coconut oil until it holds together			
Mediterranean in the Tropics	¼ c. sunflower seeds, 1/3 c. almonds	¼ c. raisins, ¼ c. dried pineapple, ¼ c. dried apricots, then ¼ c. coconut	¼ tsp. vanilla + ¼ tsp. ground cinnamon
Double	½ c. sunflower seeds, 2/3 c. almonds	½ c. raisins, ½ c. pineapple, ½ c. apricots, then ½ c. coconut	½ tsp. vanilla + ½ tsp. cinnamon
Quad	1 c. sunflower seeds, 1 1/3 c. almonds	1 c. raisins, 1 c. apricots, then 1 c. coconut	1 tsp. vanilla + 1 tsp. cinnamon
Sunny Vacation	¼ c. sunflower seeds	½ c. dates, ¼ c. dried apricots, then ¼ c. coconut	½ tsp. vanilla + 1/8 tsp. ground cinnamon
Double	½ c. sunflower seeds	1 c. dates, ½ c. dried apricots, then ½ c. coconut	1 tsp. vanilla + ¼ tsp. ground cinnamon
Quad	1 c. sunflower seeds	2 c. dates, 1 c. dried apricots, then 1 c. coconut	2 tsp. vanilla + ½ tsp. ground cinnamon

	Grind:	Add:	Stream:
Cinnamix	1/3 c. almonds, ¼ c. cashews	½ c. dates, ¼ c. raisins	1 tsp. ground cinnamon
Double	2/3 c. almonds, ½ c. cashews	1 c. dates, ½ c. raisins	2 tsp. ground cinnamon
Quad	1 1/3 c. almonds, 1 c. cashews	2 c. dates, 1 c. raisins	1 Tbs. ground cinnamon
PBJ	1/3 c. peanuts	½ c. dates, ¼ c. dried cherries	<1/4 tsp. salt + optional ½ tsp. coconut oil
Double	2/3 c. peanuts	1 c. dates, ½ c. dried cherries	<1/2 tsp. salt + optional 1 tsp. coconut oil
Quad	1 1/3 c. peanuts	2 c. dates, 1 c. dried cherries	scant tsp. salt + optional 1 tsp. coconut oil
Tropical	¼ c. almonds, 1 Tbs. cashews	½ c. dates, 1/3 c. dried pineapple, then 1/3 c. coconut	½ tsp. dried orange peel + 1-2 tsp. coconut oil + ½ tsp. vanilla
Double	½ c. almonds, 2 Tbs. cashews	1 c. dates, 2/3 c. dried pineapple, then 2/3 c. coconut	1 tsp. dried orange peel + 2-3 tsp. coconut oil + 1 tsp. vanilla
Quad	1 c. almonds, ¼ c. cashews	2 c. dates, 1 1/3 c. dried pineapple, then 1 1/3 c. coconut	2 tsp. dried orange peel + 1 Tbs. coconut oil + 2 tsp. vanilla
Gingersnap	1/3 c. almonds, ¼ c. pecans	¾ c. dates	¼-½ tsp. ginger + ¼ tsp. cinnamon + ¼ tsp. cloves
Double	2/3 c. almonds, ½ c. pecans	1 ½ c. dates	½-1 tsp. ginger + ½ tsp. cinnamon + ½ tsp. cloves
Quad	1 1/3 c. almonds, 1 c. pecans	3 c. dates	1-2 tsp. ginger + 1 tsp. cinnamon + 1 tsp. cloves
Coco-shew	1/3 c. cashews	½ c. raisins, ¼ c. coconut	½ tsp. vanilla
Double	2/3 c. cashews	1 c. raisins, ½ c. coconut	1 tsp. vanilla
Quad	1 1/3 c. cashews	2 c. raisins, 1 c. coconut	2 tsp. vanilla
Peanutty Bars	¼ c. peanuts	½ c. dates	slightly less than ¼ tsp. salt
Double	½ c. peanuts	1 c. dates	< ½ tsp. salt
Quad	1 c. peanuts	2 c. dates	scant tsp. salt
Chocolate Peanut Butter Delight	1/3 c. peanuts, 2-3 Tbs. chocolate chips or dark chocolate	½ c. dates	½ tsp. vanilla
Double	2/3 c. peanuts, ¼ c.+ chocolate chips or dark chocolate	1 c. dates	1 tsp. vanilla
Quad	1 1/3 c. peanuts, ½-2/3 c. chocolate chips or dark chocolate	2 c. dates	2 tsp. vanilla

	Grind:	Add:	Stream:
Zesty Cranberry	1/3 c. pecans	½ c. dates, 1/3 c. dried cranberries	generous ¼ tsp. vanilla + 1/8-1/4 tsp. cinnamon + ¼ tsp. dried orange peel (optional)
Double	2/3 c. pecans	1 c. dates, 2/3 c. dried cranberries	½ tsp. vanilla + ½ tsp. cinnamon + ½ tsp. dried orange peel (optional)
Quad	1 1/3 c. pecans	2 c. dates, 1 1/3 c. dried cranberries	generous tsp. vanilla + ¾-1 tsp. cinnamon + 1 tsp. dried orange peel (optional)
Bible Bars	1/3 c. walnuts	¼ c. dried figs, ½ c. dates	Squirt of honey
Double	2/3 c. walnuts	½ c. dried figs, 1 c. dates	2 squirts of honey
Quad	1 1/3 c. walnuts	1 c. dried figs, 2 c. dates	4 squirts of honey
Apple Pie	1/3 c. almonds, 1/3 c. walnuts	½ c. dates, ½ c. dried apples	1/2+ tsp. cinnamon
Double	2/3 c. almonds, 2/3 c. walnuts	1 c. dates, 1 c. dried apples	1-1 ½ tsp. cinnamon
Quad	1 1/3 c. almonds, 1 1/3 c. walnuts	2 c. dates, 2 c. dried apples	2-3 tsp. cinnamon

Popeye Bars

 Work Intensity

 Storage

Cost

Molasses is a great source of iron, but a difficult sell to kiddos. Some can stir it into yogurt, but my kids gave that a thumbs-down. Try the "big muscles" sell job with this recipe. You may use honey in place of the molasses, but then you have to call them "Energy Bars" instead of "Popeye Bars."

SF GF

Ingredients:

1 c. almonds or crispy almonds
1 c. walnuts or crispy walnuts
½ c. pine nuts OR ½ c. more walnuts
Cinnamon and nutmeg
2 tsp. unsweetened cocoa powder
Squeeze of honey as needed

½ c. unsweetened coconut
¼ c. mini chocolate chips
½ c. raisins
¼ c. unsulphured blackstrap molasses
¼ c. maple syrup

Method:

Preheat oven to 250 degrees F. Lightly coat a rimmed cookie sheet or 9"x13" glass baking dish with butter or oil, or use a baking stone or parchment paper. Using a food processor or blender, grind all the nuts into meal (very finely chopped). Pour into a large bowl and add the spices to taste and cocoa powder. Mix well and add the coconut, chocolate chips, raisins, molasses and maple syrup. (It's possible to simply use the food processor to combine as well.)

If it's not sticky enough to stay together, add honey until you reach a good consistency. Transfer to the cookie sheet. Spread out until even and press firmly. If it gets thinner than about ¼", push the mixture toward one side of the cookie sheet and cover any unused portion of the sheet with foil to prevent burning. Bake 40-50 minutes for chewy bars, or about 60 minutes for crunchier. Do not overbake – molasses tastes terrible if it's scorched.

Remove from oven, let cool, and cut into 2"x3" bars. A pizza cutter works great! Store in the refrigerator, either individually wrapped or in the glass dish with a lid. (OR you can dehydrate at 135F for 7-36 hours, depending on how thick they are.)

Makes about 16 bars

Protein Bars

Work Intensity

Storage

Cost

I can practically taste peanut butter no-bake cookies when I make these protein-packed, kid-friendly bars. Yum! You really can't taste the molasses, so it's a great way to get some iron into the kiddos.

SF GF 🚫 S

Ingredients:

2 c. pecans (or your favorite nut)
½ c. pine nuts or walnuts
¼ c. unsweetened coconut
¼ c. chocolate chips (optional)
2 tsp. cocoa powder, optional

2/3 c. natural creamy peanut butter
3 Tbs. unsulphured blackstrap molasses
2 Tbs. raw honey
¼ tsp. vanilla
Splash maple syrup or honey, as needed

Method:

Preheat oven to 250 degrees F. Grind nuts in food processor until they have a mealy texture. Pour into a large bowl and add coconut, chocolate chips, and cocoa. Add peanut butter, molasses, honey, and vanilla and stir well to combine. The mixture should be wet enough to just stick together, but not too gooey. Add a splash of maple syrup or honey if it's too dry.

Lightly grease a rimmed baking sheet (a silicone mat or parchment paper helps), a 9x13" glass pan, or baking stone. Pour nut mixture into pan; using wet hands, press into a flat layer, all to one side. Cover any part of the pan that does not have bars on it with foil to prevent burning. Bake for 45-60 minutes, or until just golden around the edges (OR dehydrate at 135F for 7-36 hours). The bars do not have to be dry or crispy to be done; remember that there are no eggs. Allow to cool, then cut into bars with a pizza cutter or sharp knife. Store in the refrigerator, individually wrapped or in a container (they also manage well at room temp for day trips).
Makes 16 2x3" bars

 Timesaver: Make the Popeye Bars at the same time, or just leave everything in the food processor and pulse to combine, rather than using a large bowl.

 Soaked Option: You can of course use crispy nuts, OR even soaked nuts that have not been dried out. (See resources page for how to: http://bit.ly/ZFeIvb)

⭐ **Added Bonus:** If you think the molasses taste is strong in the Popeye Bars from the previous page, the peanut butter masks the molasses excellently in this one.

Almond Power Bars

Work Intensity   Storage   Cost

Want a snack that passes for a dessert in taste but registers "way healthy" on the nutrition scale? Don't let the pricey ingredients scare you; a little bar will satisfy because they're so rich.

Ingredients:

½ c. virgin coconut oil
2 c. almonds (raw or crispy nuts)
½ c. flax meal
½ c. shredded, unsweetened coconut
½ c. unsalted almond butter
½ tsp. salt

1-2 Tbs. honey
1 Tbs. maple syrup
2-3 tsp. vanilla extract

a few squares dark chocolate, less than half a bar OR a handful of chocolate chips (optional)

Method:

In a small sauce pan, melt coconut oil over very low heat. Meanwhile, process the almonds in a food processor until chopped small. Add the flax meal, shredded coconut, almond butter and salt and pulse briefly until combined. (If you're starting with whole flax seeds, be sure to make them into a fine meal before adding to the mixture.)

Remove coconut oil from stove, and stir sweeteners and vanilla into oil. Add the liquid mixture to food processor and pulse until a coarse paste is formed. Press mixture firmly into an 8x8" glass pan.

Refrigerate for at least one hour until mixture hardens. Use the saucepan from the coconut oil and another larger one to make a pseudo double boiler by adding water to the larger pot and nesting the smaller inside it. Melt the chocolate over low heat, stirring continuously. Spread melted chocolate over the bars, then chill again until the chocolate hardens. To serve, cut into bars. Store in the refrigerator.

Makes 20 small bars

Timesaver: Use your food processor to chop nuts for baking and freeze them before you make the bars. Make power bars (p. 26) at the same time or another sweet treat like Chocomole (p. 77).

 Added Bonus: If you don't like or can't chew whole nuts, these are perfect. The almond flavor isn't overwhelming, and they're a hit with kiddos, too!

 FAQs

- ✔ *Are there any substitutes for ingredients?* **You can sub peanut butter for almond butter,** which is less expensive and often more likely to be stocked in your pantry. The taste changes, naturally, but is still excellent. It's also possible to **sub butter for coconut oil.**
- ✔ *What is virgin coconut oil?* Low temp processed coconut oil with full flavor and aroma of coconuts. Coconut oil is perhaps one of the more divisive fats/oils out there, because the mainstream puts it at the very top of the "bad fats" list, while the traditional foodie folks seek it out as the healthiEST of fats. For more information on the debate, please check out KitchenStewardship.com.
- ✔ *Can I skip the chocolate?* These bars are still mouthwatering without the chocolate but certainly less indulgent. When using almond butter that is not roasted, you may find you really appreciate the flavor boost from the chocolate.
- ✔ *I don't have a food processor. Can I use a blender?* I haven't tried the blender, but you'd just have to get the nuts chopped really small, and perhaps remove the mixture for the final mashing together, because likely the blender won't be able to keep everything moving.
- ✔ *Be sure to take care with flax meal.* It needs to be stored properly. Flax oil is extremely unstable and goes rancid quickly. Purchase it only in refrigerated sections in opaque containers. You'll often see it in the vitamin aisles – stay away from that stuff! It goes rancid 6 weeks after pressing, so watch expiration dates carefully, especially before purchasing. It should have a sweet, nutty flavor. Never cook with flax oil! It oxidizes at extremely low temps (for an oil). Only add to cold foods or foods after they have been cooked.

Adapted from Elana's Pantry (http://www.elanaspantry.com/power-bars/)

Butternut Spice Bars

Work Intensity   Storage   Cost

Incredibly simple ingredients become a simple but tasty pumpkin pie style snack bar. A great way to get veggies in during the day! My son was pumped that I allowed these to come in his lunchbox.

Ingredients

- 4 eggs
- 1 c. pureed butternut (or similar) squash, pumpkin, or sweet potato
- 2 tsp. cinnamon
- 1 Tbs. melted butter or coconut oil
- 2 Tbs. real maple syrup

Method

Separate eggs. Whip egg whites until fluffy.

In a separate bowl, combine egg yolks, squash, cinnamon, butter/oil and maple syrup. Mix well.

Fold in egg whites. Pour into a well-buttered 8x8-inch pan. Bake 35-40 minutes in a preheated 350°F oven, uncovered. A knife inserted in the center should come out clean when done.

Let cool completely. Slice into small squares. Store in the refrigerator; lasts 1-2 weeks.

Makes 12-16 bars.

 Timesaver: Use the lazy way: don't separate the eggs. Just beat everything together well. In fact, I've been known to make the batter right in the pan. I've even made them twice in the same pan after we finished one batch rather quickly and I still had sweet potato puree around...

Variations

Less sweetener: To fit with GAPS, you can skip the sweetener altogether and serve with extra butter on top.

Alternative sweeteners: Try 5-10 drops of pure stevia extract OR use honey in place of the maple syrup.

Pumpkin pie variation: Substitute the cinnamon for traditional pumpkin pie spice (1 tsp. cinnamon, ½ tsp. ginger, ¼ tsp. allspice or cloves (or both!), ¼ tsp. nutmeg – makes just over 2 tsp. to use in the recipe).

 FAQs

✓ *Can I serve this as a dessert?* Why not? Add a little whipped cream, and as long as folks are looking for something healthy with a little sweetness, as opposed to the standard sugary dessert, they won't be disappointed.

Notes from the Kitchen

✓ *Substitution ideas:* Feel free to use any orange vegetable, from pumpkin (even canned would work) to other squashes (buttercup are very sweet and mild) to sweet potatoes.

✓ *From a recipe tester:* "I was surprised that so few ingredients could taste so good. Definitely a keeper, we served it to guests and they agreed. Fast and easy, not complicated, time consuming or challenging in any way, easy enough to teach to kids. Smooth and creamy like a 'pumpkin quiche.'"

Adapted from http://kamisniche.blogspot.com/

Crispy Roasted Chickpeas

Work Intensity

Storage

Cost

These little babies may well be the perfect snack: sweet, salty (or both), crunchy, packable, no grains, low fat (for those who still think that's important), plus actual nutrition. Most importantly, did I mention salty and crunchy? Bliss.

Ingredients

Chickpeas,
> (aka garbanzo beans) dried OR canned

Extra virgin olive oil, coconut oil, or liquid oil of your choice

for every one cup cooked beans (double these amounts for one whole can)

- *Cinnasweet:* 2 tsp. sugar/sucanat/honey + ¾ tsp. cinnamon + ¼ tsp. salt
- *Pumpkin pie:* 1 tsp. cinnamon + ¼ tsp. ginger + dash cloves + ¼ tsp. salt
- *Mexican:* 2 tsp. taco seasoning + ¼-½ tsp. salt (if salt-free seasoning)
- *Spicy Yum:* 2 tsp. chili powder + ¼ tsp. salt (cut in half for less spicy)
- *Cool Ranch:* 1-2 tsp. ranch dressing mix + ¼-½ tsp. salt
- *Italian blend:* 2 tsp. Italian seasoning (+ ½ tsp. salt, optional)

Salty note: if your canned beans are already salted, decrease salt in the seasonings.
Sweet Note: when using sweetener, avoid higher temperatures or the sweets will burn. See FAQs for a note on sucanat.

My Story

I've been trying to pin down the perfect way to make "crispy roasted chickpeas," a craze that apparently took over the blogosphere in early 2009 when I didn't know what was going on. I've done them slowly, quickly, and burnt to a crisp. I've used the toaster oven and the regular oven. I've tried canned and home-cooked beans, oiled at the beginning, seasoned at the end, and more.

If I've learned one thing, it's that every oven is different, and there are a lot of sizes of chickpeas out there.

So please don't hate me when I say "10-30 minutes." I know that's a big difference, but I'd hate to have you break a tooth on your crispy roasted chickpeas because they were tiny and went beyond crispy. You know?

You might have to burn your tongue a little tasting the chickpeas until you learn the best timing for your oven and your beans...but it will be worth it. Write everything down in my handy little chart, and when you nail the perfect temp and timing for your kitchen....don't ever move or get a new stove. You'll have discovered the perfect crunchy munchy snack and won't have to think about it again!

Method

- If using canned beans, drain and rinse well.
  - See below for how to cook dry beans (under soaked option).
- Spread cooked, measured beans out on a towel and pat dry.
  - *If you have the time, it doesn't hurt to leave them for an hour or so. I liked to skip the whole towel step because I hate laundry, but just grab a clean dish towel and do it. Or skip it...but don't get mad at me if you can't get to "crispy" perfectly!*
- Choose your method: *quick or easy.*
  - If you tend to forget things in the oven, go with "easy" which includes a long, slow roast.
  - If you want to get out of the kitchen faster, choose "quick" and stick with one temperature, lots of stirring, and some taste testing.

After a dry roast according to your speed preference below, here's

How to oil and season your beans:
- Add about a half Tablespoon of olive oil per cup beans. I do a quick glug from my bottle.
- Stir to coat, then add the seasoning blend of your choice (or make something up!). Some find they like nearly doubling the seasoning.
- If you forget to stir before adding the seasoning, that's okay too. I usually end up dumping it all in together...

The Easy Way
I like this option because there's less babysitting the oven, although it takes longer overall. My house is cold in the winter, so no biggie!

1. Preheat oven to 300F. Spread the cooked, patted dry beans on a rimmed baking sheet, lined with a mat or parchment paper if you prefer. *Don't overfill your baking sheet – I know it's tempting! Also, a baking stone is wonderful for attaining crispiness, but only use one if it has edges. Too many beans jump ship without them.*

2. Roast for one hour in a toaster or regular oven, stirring every 20-30 minutes.

You'll notice the beans starting to dry out, but they're nowhere near crispy at this point. If you have an oven *full* of beans, you might even give them an extra 15-30 minutes at 300 degrees to get more dried out.

3. Turn the oven up to 400F.

4. Pour the warm-but-not-yet-crispy beans into a bowl (here's where you're happy you chose the parchment paper for speed) and follow the directions for oil and seasoning above. *Your 1-cup measuring cup comes in handy for scooping.*

5. Spread the seasoned beans back out on the baking sheet, and when the oven reaches temperature, return beans to the oven for 5-20 minutes, stirring every 5-10 minutes. *Canned beans seem to get done more quickly, only about 5 minutes at 400F.*

How do I know when they're done?

Ah, the million dollar question. Actually, considering the cost of legumes, it's probably a 79-cent question, but important for your snacking pleasure nonetheless.

You want to shoot for crunchy – no bean taste, no mealy texture whatsoever. If you recognize it as a chickpea, keep baking. The best crispy roasted chickpeas feel like pretzels in your mouth. Remember pretzels? Mmmmm...

The only problem is that you might end up eating the whole batch if you're not careful.

The other problem is that they will crisp up just a bit as they cool, so seeking perfection while your tongue is still burning may result in overcrisped chickpeas. Overdone can range from "slightly too crunchy to be truly enjoyable but still addicting in a disturbing sort of way" to "Ack! I think I broke a tooth!"

If perchance your chickpeas start popping and hitting the ceiling of your oven, they are crispy. They are roasted. They are done.

The golden rule: It's always easier to toast a bit longer than to un-toast, which is, of course, impossible.

Please see FAQs for notes on different types of pans before you make burnt-to-a-crisp chickpeas.

The Quick Way
For those of you who would rather get it over with...

Toaster oven: (most fit 1-2 cups garbanzo beans) Simply bake about 20-40 minutes at 375F. Feel free to oil and season at the beginning of the process, although I think you taste the seasoning more if you dry roast for the first 15 minutes, then stir the seasoning and oil on, then toast the final part in sets of 5 minutes.

Full sized oven: Preheat to 375F. Bake 30-55 minutes until crispy. You can either oil and season at the beginning or dry roast, removing after 25 minutes to season, then returning to the oven for 5-25 minutes.

Store in an airtight container at room temperature once completely cooled. If you're worried that you underbaked them, go ahead and store in the refrigerator and bake again the next time your oven is on anyway.

They last a really long time...except they probably won't stick around very long unless you hide them!

Note: If you are feeling plucky and trust yourself to really watch them, a few testers preferred roasting at 425F...but the times ranged from 20-50 minutes! See what I mean about ovens and beans varying? Also, this temp is a big high for sweetened beans.

 Added Bonus: Both nut-free and gluten-free, a rare find in a crunchy snack!

Healthy Upgrades

Soaked option: If for reasons of frugality, avoiding BPA in cans, and nutrition, you want to cook your own garbanzos:

1. Rinse dry beans. I never cook less than a pound of beans because it doesn't seem worth the energy usage. Go for two pounds, if you ask me (see FAQs for ideas to use them all up).
2. Cover with double the amount of water as beans (140F temperature optimal).
3. Soak overnight or for at least 12 hours.
4. Pour off water and rinse beans again.
5. For optimal flatulence reduction, change the soaking water once or twice (soaking in between) before moving on to the next step.
6. Cover with ample water and bring to a boil.
7. Skim off any weird foam at the top.
8. Cook on medium low, uncovered, for the first hour.
9. Cover and cook for 4ish more hours or until beans feel cooked when squished.
10. Note: keep in mind that chickpeas need to keep their shape well, so don't wait until "mush" and avoid adding baking soda which can make "mush" happen. If you wish to add salt, wait until nearly cooked. Adding salt too early can cause tough, hard beans.

FAQs

✓ *What do I do if the roasted chickpeas aren't exactly "crispy"?* It's easy to fix undertoasted beans (not so much overcooked, so shoot low!): Retoast your cooled beans in a preheated oven (or toaster oven) at 350F for 5-10 minutes. Taste test, write down what you did, and repeat if not quite there yet.
✓ *What if I cook too many beans?*
  o Put extra beans in a cold grain salad (p. 73) or lettuce salad, make soup, or toss them into homemade rice dishes (more here: http://bit.ly/ZFeIvb)
  o 10 options online (http://bit.ly/TsgWKE), from Morocan to garam marsala.

- 15 more ideas online (http://bit.ly/U2uiMd)
✓ *Can I freeze cooked beans?* Yes! They freeze great. I measure 2-cup portions before freezing, then I can just dump them into a recipe once thawed.
✓ *Can I make crispy roasted chickpeas with previously frozen beans?* Yes. Just make sure they're fully thawed before starting, and don't skip that "dry on a towel" step.
✓ *What are those little skins that come off when I dry the beans?* That's just the hull or skin, the part that's hardest to digest anyway. If you rub the chickpeas around in the towel, many of them will come off. Just pitch them.
✓ *How do I adjust the time for different pans?* Parchment paper, silicone mats and glass or ceramic dishes should work with the times given, but if you have **a dark-colored baking sheet**, reduce the times at higher temps by 25-50%. Even a light-colored, metal baking sheet may require you to shave a few minutes off the final toasting time.
✓ *My sucanat all fell off the beans. What gives?* Good point. That does happen. I just couldn't figure out where to address the problem until the FAQs. To use sucanat, you need to blend it up a bit to make it more like a powdered sugar. If that's too much work, just use honey and don't let the temp get too high.
✓ *Do you make your own ranch dressing mix?* Here is a bonus recipe for you:

Ranch Dressing Mix
Mix together (all dried):
> 2 Tbs. dill
> 2 Tbs. parsley
> 2 Tbs. chives
> 4 Tbs onion powder
> ¼-½ tsp. cayenne pepper
> 2-3 tsp. black pepper
> optional: 3-6 tsp. garlic powder (or use fresh garlic in dressing)
> optional: 2-4 tsp. salt (salt to taste if not including)

And to make actual ranch dressing with this? Use 1 ½ tsp. mix with ¾ c. mayo and ½ c. sour cream. Add a Tbs of red wine vinegar and 2 cloves real crushed garlic for a more rounded out flavor.

The problem with this particular ranch mix recipe and crispy roasted chickpeas is that the parsley and chives are too large to really stick to the beans. I might recommend making a small batch of seasoning mix without them just for this snack: ½ tsp. dill, 1 tsp. onion powder, ½ tsp. garlic powder, ¼ tsp. pepper, ¼ tsp. salt for one cup beans.

✓ *Can I make my own blends?* Why certainly, my dears. Just remember that the salt almost always makes it better, even with the sweet blends. Here are a few other ideas from the recipe testers to stir your creative juices:
  * ¾ tsp. cinnamon, ¾ tsp. coriander, 1/8 tsp. garlic powder, ½ tsp. salt
  * 1 ½ tsp. smoked paprika, ½ tsp. salt
  * 2 tsp. garlic powder, ½ tsp. salt
✓ *Do you make your own taco seasoning?* Why yes, I do. It's salt free, right here: http://bit.ly/U2uA5M
✓ *Will they give me gas?* Well...yeah...probably. Just make sure you make enough to share with everyone around you!

Handy Dandy Crispy Chickpea Chart

Date	Temperature	Time	Temp 2	Time 2	Results

Wheat Thin Style Crackers

Work Intensity

Storage

Cost

Great crackers are both thin and salty. With a hint of sweetness from vanilla that you'll never know is there, these crackers really do taste like the name brand they are imitating. Your eaters will be amazed, and you might not be able to make them fast enough!

Ingredients:

1 ¼ c. whole wheat flour
1 ½ Tbs. sugar (or honey)
½ tsp. salt
¼ tsp. paprika

4 Tbs. cold butter
¼ c. water
¼ tsp. vanilla
salt for topping

Method:

Combine the flour, sugar, salt and paprika in a medium bowl. Cut the cold butter into 1" pieces and cut into the flour mixture with a pastry blender, two knives or a food processor until evenly distributed. Combine the water and vanilla and add to the flour mixture, mixing until smooth. (Note: If you use honey, mix it in with the water.) If you need a little more water, you can add it, but be conservative.

Preheat the oven to 400 degrees F. Plan to use parchment paper or a silicone baking mat on cookie sheets, or use a baking stone and roll out the crackers right on it (not heated). Rolling directly on your surface saves a major step.

Divide the dough into 3-4 pieces and keep the other pieces covered while you work with one at a time. Lightly flour your surface or baking stone and roll the piece of dough into a large rectangle that generally fits your baking stone or cookie sheet. Roll as thinly as possible, keeping the surface and pin well floured to avoid sticking. Flip the dough often. Move the entire piece of flat dough to your baking surface (if necessary), then cut into cracker shapes (1 ½" x 1 ½" is great) with a pizza cutter or sharp knife. (Do not cut with sharp knives on silicone mats.) You do not need to leave space between. If you trim the edges flat, roll all the trimmings together at once rather than adding to the next ball of dough, or else they'll get too tough.

Sprinkle lightly with salt – do not skip this step! – and bake for 5-10 minutes until crisp and lightly browned. Baking stones take a bit longer. Watch them closely as the crackers can go from lightly browned to *toast* quickly. Repeat with remaining dough.

Remove the crackers from the oven and cool on the pan or on a plate; they cool quickly. These crackers will stay crisp for many days, but are best stored in airtight containers. You can also freeze them.

OR

Just bake them for 5-6 minutes, and even if they're still soft, turn off the oven and leave the crackers in while the oven cools. In a few hours or overnight, you'll have perfectly crispy, crumble in your mouth crackers!

Note: electric ovens continue to generate heat after being turned off, so if you're on electric, check the crackers for extra browning after 10 minutes or so. Alternately, head the problem off at the pass by holding the oven door open a minute after you turn of the heat.

Makes a bit more than one average sized box of crackers

 Timesaver: Make a double batch of dough and refrigerate or freeze half, then roll out and bake later. You can bake a quick batch while making a dinner that uses the oven, have fresh crackers and just turn the oven on once.

 Added Bonus: You will be a hero. Everybody loves these crackers, and if you roll them out and cut on the baking surface, they might not even look homemade.

Healthy Upgrades:

S **Soaked option:** To soak these crackers, just make the dough as directed above except with whey in place of the water. Allow to sit at room temperature 12-24 hours. Salt may inhibit the soaking process, so you can omit the salt and incorporate it right before rolling out if you choose. Simple!

 ## FAQs

✔ *Why not put the crackers right on the cookie sheet?* I HIGHLY recommend using a baking stone or at least parchment paper or a Nonstick Silicone Baking Mat. Because I can roll the dough right out on the stone or mat before baking, I don't have to worry about rumpled crackers as I move the fragile dough. People say, "Those are homeMADE?" because most of my crackers have perfect shape and are sooooo delectably thin. Plus, crackers stuck to a baking sheet just makes a mess.

✔ *How do I know when they're done?* You want them to be almost crispy, but not totally breakable, to deem them "done," because they will crisp up a bit as they cool. You'll learn after a tray or two the difference between "too soft" "done" and "oops." They're still tasty when they're soft, just not so cracker-y.

✔ *What if the crackers on the edge are done but the center is still soft?* Just remove the crispy crackers and give the others a few more minutes.

Adapted from the King Arthur Flour Whole Grain Baking Cookbook

Whole Wheat Graham Crackers

Work Intensity

Storage

Cost

I can't tell you how many times I've been asked if I have a homemade graham cracker recipe. This one knocks on the door of being a sugar cookie...but it's better than a box!

Ingredients

2 ½ c. white whole wheat flour
½ c. dark brown sugar OR ¾ c. sucanat
1 tsp. baking soda
¾ tsp. salt
1 ½ tsp. cinnamon
½ c. (1 stick) unsalted butter, cut and frozen
1/3 c. honey
1/3 c. whole milk
2 Tbs. whey
4 tsp. vanilla

Method

Prep: cut the butter into chunks and freeze.

Mix the flour, sugar, baking soda, salt and cinnamon in a food processor. Add the butter and pulse or mix until the mixture is crumbly.

In a separate bowl, whisk the honey, milk, whey, and vanilla. Pour into the food processor and pulse or mix slowly until the dough just comes together.

Flour your hands and form the (very sticky) dough into a flat disk, then chill in the refrigerator in some sort of airtight container for at least two hours or up to three days, depending on your schedule.

When you're ready to bake, prep two baking stones or cookie sheets with parchment paper, and move the oven racks to the top and bottom positions. Preheat the oven to 350F.

Divide the dough into two portions, returning one to the fridge. This is a very sticky dough, so keeping it cold is vital to your rolling success.

Flour the parchment paper and roll out half the dough to about 1/8" thick, using flour as necessary (and it will be). Parchment paper on top is quite helpful, too. Repeat with the other half.

With a pizza cutter or sharp knife, cut the dough to make crackers in your desired size. To mimic boxed crackers as closely as possible, make light dent lines down the center of each cracker and use a skewer or toothpick to make the cute little holes. Sprinkle the tops with additional sugar if desired.

Bake at 350F for about 8 minutes, then swap the trays from top to bottom and bake 8 minutes more. When the edges are browning and beginning to get crispy to the touch, turn the oven off, but leave the crackers inside. As the oven cools down, the crackers will crisp up. The first time you do this, and *especially* if you have an electric oven (which will continue to generate heat after you turn it off), check every 5-10 minutes or so to make sure the crackers aren't burning.

Finish cooling on racks if necessary and store at room temperature in airtight containers. Freeze to preserve crispiness if you want to hang onto them more than a week, but we've proven that they'll last more months than you would imagine.

Makes about 2 dozen 2x2" squares.

 Added Bonus: You bet you can use these guys for S'mores!

Healthy Upgrades

Soaked option: This is a pretty easy recipe to soak. Simply omit the baking soda and salt when you mix up the dough, then allow it to sit at room temperature for 12-24 hours.

After soaking, sprinkle the baking soda and salt evenly over the surface of the dough, folding in half while sprinkling if you can, to make sure it gets incorporated as uniformly as possible. Fold and knead the dough to incorporate, then refrigerate at least two hours before baking. Alternately, you can refrigerate the dough first, then add the baking soda and salt. Proceed with rolling the dough as described above.

Note: Adding the baking soda and salt is definitely an extra step, and one that annoys me and potentially makes the crackers less light and crispy because the dough gets overworked. For my own purposes, I'd rather risk some phytic acid than bother with kneading the dough twice, so I just mix up the dough as written, soak on the counter 24 hours, refrigerate, and roll out.

FAQs

- ✓ *Could I make shapes with the crackers?* Absolutely. Use simple cookie cutters without much detail, since the crackers puff up quite a bit and would lose any intricate designs anyway. If you separate smaller crackers on the baking sheet, only bake 10-12 minutes, and keep a close eye on them.
- ✓ *Why are the crackers puffing up so much???* Don't be scared. They just do that. They'll calm down when they're cooled.
- ✓ *What if I don't have dark brown sugar?* Really, regular brown sugar (or sucanat) does just fine.
- ✓ *Where do I get whey?* Check the resources page at http://bit.ly/ZFelvb for directions.
- ✓ *Do you lick your fingers when you make these?* Yeah, maybe. Did you?
- ✓ *Can I skip the parchment paper?* Don't dream of it. I *never* need parchment paper on my baking stones, and I often roll out other cracker recipes right on the stone. Not this one. I was scraping off graham cracker crumbs for half an hour. Don't try it!
- ✓ *Are these actually healthy?* All right, you caught me — there's quite a bit of sweetener in these crackers, isn't there? Believe it or not, the original recipe called for a whole cup of brown sugar. They're still quite good with half a cup, but if you're making them for kids who expect a sweet treat, go ahead and double it. Just don't tell them I told you to!
- ✓ *Got a gluten-free, dairy-free version?* My colleague Erin does, right here: http://bit.ly/UauBui

Recipe adapted from Heartland Renaissance (http://bit.ly/WnoODd) and reprinted with permission.

Old-Fashioned Stovetop Popcorn

Work Intensity   Storage   Cost

When I read that microwave popcorn was on the list of seven things the "experts" won't eat, it confirmed that I was doing an important thing in making my own, something I had never done before my real food journey began. Homemade popcorn is just as portable as the bagged up stuff you can buy at a store, but without random additives.

Ingredients:

Coconut oil, refined or unrefined
          or butter
Whole popcorn
Salt

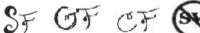

Method:

Melt enough coconut oil (best choice) or butter (keep the temp very low so it doesn't scorch) to completely cover the bottom of your chosen pot, but not more than 1/8". Too much oil will make for soggy popcorn. A pot with a glass lid is the most fun! *Even with unrefined coconut oil, I never really taste the coconut flavor.*

Place one kernel of popcorn in the oil and heat over medium high, covered of course, until that kernel pops. Pour in more popcorn until either the bottom of your pot is covered with a roomy single layer or you have enough, whichever comes first. About ½ cup dry popcorn is usually plenty for a family of four (unless popcorn is for dinner, ahem) and fills a 4-quart pot.

Wiggle the pot to coat all the kernels and pop over medium high heat. Yes, please cover the pot! Jiggle the pot back and forth every 30 seconds or so to keep things moving around in there. Just like microwave popcorn, you'll hear the popping slow down when it's time to remove the pot from the heat.

Meanwhile, melt a few tablespoons (or more) of butter in a separate pot. OR to save dishes, put the popped corn in a bowl, wipe out the remaining kernels and melt butter in the popping pot. Pour butter over the popcorn and salt to taste. Yum!

The last time I made popcorn, I overdid the amount and ended up with way too much. I just left it, dry, in the pot, and two weeks later I was still enjoying a piece here and there as a drive-by snack. Don't know what that is? Wander through your kitchen and see if there's anything in your mouth after your "drive-by"!

Tater Skin Crispies

Work Intensity

Storage

Cost

Free is a great deal. Reclaim something that most people toss out, take three minutes, and you've got a snack to go that is a bit like a potato chip, but loads healthier.

SF GF CF (no soy) (no wheat) (no shellfish)

Ingredients:

Potato peels, either from
        baked or raw potatoes
Extra Virgin Olive Oil (EVOO)
Salt and pepper

Method:

Be sure to scrub your potatoes well, as you would for bakers. Whether you peel them for mashed potatoes or bake and then peel for potato salad, save the skins. No time right away? They'll hold in the refrigerator for you for a few days. Next time you're turning the oven on, drizzle EVOO over the skins and toss with salt and pepper to taste. Garlic powder or other herbs and seasonings work great, too, but aren't necessary.

If you're not very flexible in the kitchen, you're going to hate this next part, but bear with me. It's free, so even if you mess it up, you're not out much. Spread in a single layer on a cookie sheet, preferably lined with parchment paper or a silicone baking mat, and put in the oven. If you've got something going for dinner, bake at that temperature. At 350 degrees F, they'll take 15-20 minutes, or about 10-12 at 425 F. Sometimes I'll put them in for the last 10 minutes of the dinner meal at 350 then pump up the temperature to 425 for 5 minutes to really crisp them up. They're done when they look brown around the edges, are slightly crunchy, and taste awesome!

IF there are any left over, you can store them in an airtight container either on the counter or in the fridge. When I toast just the peels with zero potato attached (from peeling already baked potatoes), they're not quite as flavorful, so I tend to crumble them on top of salads for a crunchy touch – a great gluten-free substitute for croutons.

 Timesaver: Peel directly onto the baking sheet and drizzle EVOO right there to save a bowl.

 Added Bonus: My kids truly think these are potato chips. Yes!

Take-Along Spelt Biscuits

Work Intensity   Storage   Cost

I'm always surprised when characters in historical fiction books take "biscuits" in their lunch pails. A cold, hard biscuit seems unappealing to me – I always heat my leftover dinner biscuits. Perhaps "biscuits" refers to crackers or cookies in those books, or maybe they had a recipe like this one. You really can eat them cold, on the go, with no butter or honey on top. Flaky and slightly, inexplicably sweet, each bite melts in your mouth like no other bread product I've encountered.

SF   CF   🚫SW   🚫   [S]

Ingredients

2 ¼ c. spelt flour
1 ½ tsp. baking powder
½ tsp. baking soda
¾ tsp. salt

6 Tbs. unrefined coconut oil (that's ¼ c. + 2 Tbs.)
¾ c. milk, coconut milk, nut milk, or water
1 Tbs. apple cider vinegar

Method:

Mix the dry ingredients together in a medium bowl. Using a pastry blender or two knives, cut the coconut oil (solid form, chill if it has turned to liquid) into the flour mixture until uniform, pea-sized balls of coconut oil are distributed evenly. Mix the vinegar and water together. Slowly pour the liquid into the bowl and mix to combine.

Flaky pastries like biscuits are most successful when the dough is handled as little as possible. Try pouring a bit of liquid in at a time, mixing until the flour is just wet, then pouring more liquid in another part of the bowl and repeating the process.

On a floured board or a baking stone, roll out or press the dough to about ½" thick. Using a sharp knife or pizza cutter, make 2"x2" squares. Transfer to a lightly greased cookie sheet, silicone baking mat or ungreased baking stone to bake, leaving a bit of space in between each biscuit. In a preheated 450 degrees F oven, bake for 10-14 minutes until golden brown and flaky in the middle.

Makes 12-14 biscuits

 Added Bonus: If you've been afraid to try spelt flour, I guarantee this is a certain-success recipe for your first experiment!

Healthy Upgrades: :

Soaked option: You can either make the dough as written and leave it to sit on the counter overnight, or you can omit the baking soda, powder, and salt for the Nourishing Traditions soak then add those just before baking. (Some say that sodium inhibits the soaking process.) Sprinkle the added ingredients onto the dough and make sure they get mixed in evenly without overworking the dough. The results are different either way, perhaps a little more flat if you use all the ingredients during the soak, since the rising power of the baking soda and powder are gone.

Sprouted spelt flour is also excellent in this recipe and is always my go-to biscuit when I haven't planned ahead for a meal.

FAQs

- ✔ *Will they work with other grains?* I'm afraid to try! These biscuits are *so good* with spelt, so I'm not messing with what works.
- ✔ *What's the best liquid to use?* Honestly, I prefer the result with water.
- ✔ *What is spelt flour? Where do I find it?* Spelt is simply a form of wheat, more related to ancient forms of the plant, with slightly less gluten than traditional whole wheat. You can find it at health food stores and quite often at conventional grocery stores in smaller packages. It's more expensive than regular flour, but if you buy in bulk or find the right source, the price difference isn't extreme.
- ✔ *Can I use refined coconut oil?* I believe it's the virgin coconut oil, with the flavor and aroma of coconuts, that gives these biscuits their slight sweetness. I don't taste the coconuts in the final product, but if you really, really dislike the taste of coconut, it would work with refined coconut oil as well.
- ✔ *Can I use sprouted flour so I don't have to soak?* Yes!
- ✔ *Why soak?* See the soaking grains primer on page 82.

Thank you to GNOWFGLINS for this incredible recipe!

Honey Whole Wheat Pumpkin Muffins

Work Intensity

Storage

Cost

One bowl "dump in the ingredients" simplicity, whole grain goodness, and the most moist muffin you've ever met make these our family's ultimate favorite muffin recipe. The original is for pumpkin muffins, but banana nut, applesauce and blueberry versions are included.

Ingredients:

¾ c. honey OR 1 c. sucanat or sugar
2 eggs
¼ tsp. baking powder
1 tsp. baking soda
¾ tsp. salt
½ tsp. cloves
1 Tbs. molasses (opt.)

½ tsp. cinnamon
½ tsp. nutmeg
1 2/3 c. whole wheat flour*
½ c. melted butter or coconut oil
¼ c. cold water
1 c. pumpkin (about half a 15 oz can)

*I usually use "white whole wheat flour" for muffins.

Method:

Mix all ingredients together. Put in greased loaf pan or muffin tin. Bake at 325 degrees:

- Bread (one loaf) = 75-90 minutes
- 12 Muffins = 45 minutes (with honey, only 35-40 minutes)
- 24-30 Mini muffins = 25 minutes

Variations:

- ✔ *Banana Nut*: Use 2 bananas plus applesauce to equal one cup in place of pumpkin, add ½ cup chopped walnuts, delete cloves and nutmeg.
- ✔ *Banana-Cran:* As above but add ½ c. chopped cranberries, fresh OR dried.
- ✔ *Applesauce Spice:* Use natural applesauce in place of the pumpkin.
- ✔ *Blueberry:* Same as above and add ½-1 cup blueberries, delete cinnamon and cloves.

Serving suggestion: Best served with unpasteurized fresh Michigan cider straight from the farm...but if you're not as lucky as I am, any apple cider will have to do. Or just a glass of milk or water; you can't really mess these guys up.

Healthy Upgrades:

 Sprouted spelt flour is also marvelous in these muffins.

Soaked option:

Mix together and allow to rest (soak) overnight at room temperature:

> 1 2/3 c. white whole wheat flour
> 1 c. pureed pumpkin
> ¾ c. water + 2 Tbs buttermilk or plain yogurt
> ½ c. melted butter or coconut oil, allowed to cool slightly before mixing in

When ready to bake, add:

> 1 c. natural granular sweetener OR ¾ c. honey
> 2 eggs   ½ tsp. baking powder
> 1 ½ tsp. baking soda   ¾ tsp. salt
> ½ tsp. cloves   ½ tsp. cinnamon
> ½ tsp. nutmeg

Method: Pour into muffin cups and bake 45 minutes at 325 degrees F (35-40 with honey). They may be a bit more moist than you're used to with the "toothpick test". Do not overbake! Allow to rest 5 minutes in the tins, then tip out to cool on racks.

FAQs

- ✔ *Can I use home-pureed pumpkin?* Yes, and it's absolutely wonderful. Just be sure that you've drained some water out so things aren't too moist.
- ✔ *Can I use other orange vegetables?* As with most orange veggie recipes, this one adapts well to squash or sweet potato.
- ✔ *What do I do with the rest of the canned pumpkin?* Try Healthy Pumpkin Cookies (with various levels of nutrition, just like this recipe) or Low-carb Pumpkin Pancakes or Cabbage Pumpkin Soup.
- ✔ *For more FAQs and recipes, check out the online page http://bit.ly/ZFeIvb*
- ✔ *Why soaked?* See the Soaking Grains Primer on p. 82.

Get more soaked grain recipes with a FREE 85-page ebook online under eBooks heading at http://www.KitchenStewardship.com

Whole Wheat Banana Flax Muffins

Work Intensity   Storage   Cost

Everybody needs a handful of recipes to default to when the bananas get brown. Here is portable banana bread with a twist: flax seed, a healthy fat that can be tricky to use.

Ingredients

1 ½ c. whole wheat pastry flour (or traditional or white whole wheat)

¾ c. ground flax seed

1 tsp. baking soda

½ c. sugar or sucanat OR ¼ c. honey

1 whole egg

½ c. melted coconut oil or butter

1 c. mashed, overripe bananas

1 tsp. vanilla extract

2 Tbs. plain yogurt

½ c. chopped walnuts (optional)

Method:

In a large mixing bowl, mix together flour, flax, baking soda, and sugar. In a separate bowl, mix egg, oil, bananas, vanilla, and yogurt. Mix the wet ingredients into the dry and stir to combine. Fold in walnuts.

Use paper muffin cups or spray the muffin pans with non-stick spray. Bake large muffins 20-25 minutes (or mini muffins for about 15 minutes) at 350 degrees in a preheated oven.

Store at room temperature for a day or two, but for any longer they should be refrigerated because of the delicate oils in flax and the whole grains.

Makes 12 muffins or 30 mini muffins.

 Added Bonus: Flax has high omega 3s and other health benefits.

 FAQs

- ✔ *Can you taste the flax?* Not really. They go over as well as any banana bread.
- ✔ *Be careful to purchase and store flax with great care.*
- ✔ *Can they be egg-free?* This recipe came from a friend whose son has an egg allergy – they work just great with the flax and water egg substitute.
- ✔ *How do I use flax in other recipes?* See the tutorial online here http://bit.ly/ZFeIvb for substituting flax.

Grain-free Coconut Muffins

Work Intensity

Storage

Cost

This was the first grain-free recipe with coconut flour I ever made, and it remains a favorite because it's so very simple and everyone loves them.

Ingredients

3 eggs
2 Tbs. unrefined coconut oil, melted
¼ c. honey or maple syrup
¼ tsp. salt
¼ c. coconut flour
¼ tsp. baking soda

   SF

Method

Preheat oven to 375F. Beat or stir eggs, coconut oil, honey and salt together until smooth. Be sure to mix the oil in immediately as it will likely solidify as soon as it hits the cold eggs. Sift coconut flour into the batter and sprinkle baking soda over the top so that it mixes in evenly. Beat or whisk hard until smooth.

I highly recommend using muffin cup liners for this recipe, but if you don't mind the clean-up, you can grease 6 muffin cups with coconut oil. Divide batter evenly between 6 cups (usually about halfway full) and bake at 375F for 10-12 minutes until a toothpick in the center comes out clean and tops are springy, not mushy.

Remove to a wire rack to cool. Store at room temperature 3-5 days.

Makes 6 muffins.

Variations

Alternative sweeteners: I often use half maple syrup and half honey; I like the way the flavors balance out. I've also successfully used both date sugar and sucanat, so I'm pretty confident any granulated sweetener will work as well. Simply whisk in after the egg/coconut oil and before the coconut flour. Sucanat makes a considerably darker muffin, but just as tasty.

Make additions: Try ½ tsp. cinnamon and a handful of raisins for cinnamon raisin. This basic recipe is a pretty blank palate for adding all sorts of things: blueberries, dried fruits, shredded coconut on top, chocolate chips – have fun making new muffins every time you bake!

 Timesaver: My easy trick to melt coconut oil: I always leave it in a glass jar on my stove, which means if I'm lucky, something is already cooking and it's melted. If not, put the jar near the oven vent while the oven is preheating, and you should have 2 Tbs. melted within 5 minutes. To speed up the process even more, place your measured coconut oil in a muffin tin in the oven while it preheats, or even skip melting the coconut oil, as long as it's pretty soft.

 ## FAQs

- ✓ *Can I double it?* I usually do; a half dozen disappears far too quickly!

- ✓ *What if I don't have coconut oil?* I'm sure butter would work just fine.

- ✓ *What is unrefined coconut oil?* That's the one that tastes and smells like coconuts. It adds a bit of sweetness to the recipe as well.

Notes from the Kitchen

If you have empty muffin cups in your tin, put a bit of water in the bottom of each one to help the muffins bake evenly and come out moist.

The muffin batter is very runny at first. If you let it sit, it really, really thickens up as the coconut flour soaks up the liquids. However, the muffins will stay in the shape you plop them, and they may take longer to bake. Smooth out the tops with a spoon. I don't recommend taking a break once the batter is ready if you can help it. Have your muffin tin/paper cups prepared.

This recipe is one of my favorites to make with children because it's so very simple. There aren't a thousand ingredients, you can mix with a spoon or an electric mixer, and kids love filling muffin tins with paper liners. Let your kiddos add something different to each muffin if you'd like!

Grain-free Pumpkin Muffins

Work Intensity

Storage

Cost

Put my favorite grain-free muffins together with the famous KS pumpkin muffins, and – voila! You have these simple, delicious, grain-free wonders.

Ingredients

- 2 large eggs (or 3 medium)
- 2 Tbs. unrefined coconut oil, melted
- 2 Tbs. maple syrup
- ½ c. pumpkin or pureed squash or sweet potato
- ¼ tsp. salt
- ¼ c. coconut flour
- ¼ tsp. baking soda
- ½ tsp. cinnamon
- ½ tsp. nutmeg
- ½ tsp. cloves

Method

Preheat oven to 375F.

Beat or mix eggs, coconut oil, maple syrup, pureed orange vegetable, and salt together until smooth. Sift coconut flour into the batter and sprinkle baking soda, cinnamon, nutmeg and cloves over the top so that they mix in evenly. Beat or whisk hard until smooth.

I recommend using muffin cup liners for this recipe, but if you don't mind the clean-up, you can grease 6 muffin cups with coconut oil. Divide batter, which will be very thick, evenly between 6 cups, and bake at 375F for 22-28 minutes until the center feels springy instead of wet (the toothpick test may not work well with coconut flour).

Remove to a wire rack to cool. Store at room temperature 3-5 days.

Makes 6 muffins.

Variations

Alternative sweeteners: Feel free to try anything you like! I think two Tablespoons of just about any sweetener will do fine, but if your orange vegetable isn't very sweet, you might need three or four.

 Timesaver: These muffins don't come out of muffin tins very nicely, but for some reason they pop right out of unbleached muffin liners. I reuse the liners a couple times to be frugal. Just store the muffins without the liners and put the liners in a container for next time.

 ## FAQs

✓ *Can I double it?* I usually do; a half dozen disappears far too quickly!

✓ *What if I don't have coconut oil?* I'm sure butter would work just fine.

✓ *What is unrefined coconut oil?* That's the one that tastes and smells like coconuts. It adds a bit of sweetness to the recipe as well.

✓ *Could I make other flavors?* I've been thinking that certainly banana could be substituted one-for-one with the pumpkin, and then use whatever spices you prefer for banana bread. I bet shredded zucchini would be great, too, maybe with a few tablespoons of cocoa powder, but I haven't experimented any more yet. I bet someone will come up with some goodies!

See the original grain-free coconut muffins on p. 58 for more great tips!

Apple Flax Muffins

Work Intensity   Storage   Cost

I'm so amazed that ground flax can take the place of all the flour in these muffins. If you like a hearty, healthy muffin, you'll never miss the grains.

Ingredients

- 1 ¼ c. ground flax OR whole flax seeds
- 2 tsp. baking powder
- 1 Tbs. cinnamon
- 1 tsp. nutmeg (optional)
- ½ tsp. salt
- 1/3 c. sugar or sucanat OR ¼ c. honey
- 4 eggs
- ¼ c. melted unrefined coconut oil (or butter)
- ½ c. applesauce (see variations for substitutes)
- 1 tsp. vanilla
- 1 large apple, chopped
- ½ c. walnuts, chopped (optional)

Method

If using ground flax (meal):

Mix dry ingredients: flax, baking powder, spices, salt, and sugar. Beat the eggs and add to the dry mixture along with oil, applesauce, and vanilla (plus honey if using). Mix thoroughly. Add apples and nuts and stir to combine.

If using whole flax seeds; you'll need a decent blender for this one:

Blend eggs, oil, flax seeds, applesauce and vanilla (plus honey if using) about a minute, or as long as it takes to grind up the seeds completely. (This just about killed my blender, so I decided "good enough" when my blender just didn't want to move anymore.) The mixture will get very gummy and thick quite quickly. (*High powered blenders might want to blend the flax seeds alone first.*)

Combine baking soda, cinnamon, nutmeg, salt and sweetener separately in a bowl.

Pour wet mixture from blender into the bowl, where you can combine with dry ingredients. Add apples and nuts and stir to combine.

Do not allow the flax mixture to sit in your blender for any amount of time at any point, as the flax meal will soak up the moisture and be more and more difficult to work with.

To finish either method:

Allow fully incorporated mixture to stand 10 minutes.

Preheat oven to 350 degrees F. Line or grease muffin tins. Spoon into tins (the batter will be very thick) and bake for 18 minutes or until a toothpick inserted in the center comes out clean. (12-14 minutes for mini muffins)

Makes 18-24 large muffins or 12 large and 24 mini muffins.

Store at room temp 1-2 days or in the refrigerator for longer.

 Timesaver: Make raw applesauce in the blender first and then use it for this recipe without washing in between.

 Added Bonus: Most of us don't get enough omega-3s, but flax will help with that.

Variations

- Try an orange vegetable puree OR yogurt OR melted coconut oil in place of the applesauce. Even just water works!
- ¾ c. flax meal and ¼ c. coconut flour also works.

Applesauce (& other) Fruit Rolls

Work Intensity

Storage

Cost

Fruit Roll-Ups don't even deserve to wear the name "fruit". They fit neatly into the category Michael Pollan calls an "edible food-like product" as well as the one called "candy." Real dried fruit is expensive, because it takes a lot of fruit to make a little roll once the water has evaporated. You don't need a dehydrator or fancy equipment to make your own at home.

Ingredients

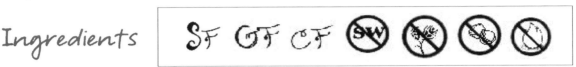

Applesauce, strawberries, or any fruit, particularly if it's past its prime.

Method:

For applesauce rolls: Spread a layer of unsweetened applesauce about ¼" thick on a piece of parchment paper or a silicone baking mat. Be sure to add cinnamon before spreading as you'll appreciate the sweetness. Try to keep the fruit/sauce as even in height as possible. Do *not* use waxed paper unless you enjoy eating waxed paper.

For any other fruit: Wash fruit and place into a blender or food processor; blend well until fully pureed, adding water if necessary but only just enough to get all the fruit incorporated into the mixture. Pour onto the baking surface as above.

Bake at 200-250F for about 2-6 hours. Check after an hour and a half, then every half hour or so until completely dried out. If perchance you begin to get impatient at 200 degrees and decide to turn up the heat, please don't become complacent as well. The rolls *will* dry out faster at higher temps and can burn on the edges. Don't allow the trays to go more than half an hour without checking them.

Be sure to rotate the pans 180 degrees every few hours, since some ovens bake unevenly back to front or side to side.

Store in an airtight container at room temperature.

 Timesaver: Make with Katie's Homemade Granola in the oven at the same time (p. 10), or do a few batches in a row on the same silicone mat to save on dishes.

 Added Bonus: You can make this with storebought natural applesauce with added cinnamon, and it's SO quick and SO easy, you'll be amazed at your savings.

✏️ FAQs

✔ *How do I know when they're done?* The rolls are done when you can lift up the end and see nothing sticky or gooey underneath. Flipping the whole roll over, if you can, may speed up the process. However, if you can peel the roll off the parchment paper or silicone mat, they're likely already done.

It's definitely possible to let fruit rolls go too long. They will get 100% crispy like chips if you do (but not nicely crunchy, just difficult to eat), and sometimes they taste a little burnt, especially on the edges. Do not leave the rolls in overnight like when you turn off the oven for granola.

✔ *Why are some fruit rolls raw food?* If you have a dehydrator or an oven that goes down to 150F, you can dry out fruit at about 135F, which preserves the enzymes of raw food. Anytime you go over 150F, you're killing enzymes. Try applesauce rolls with raw instead of cooked apples.

  ✔ *Raw applesauce*: place cored and unpeeled apples in a food processor. Only fill about half at a time. Process until everything is shredded, then scrape down and add 2-4 Tbs. water and a heavy sprinkle of cinnamon. Process again, likely adding another 2-4 Tbs. water through the top and scraping down one more time.

✔ *How long will dried fruit rolls last?* If no moisture is introduced, dried fruit lasts a very long time, at least a year.

✔ *Can I use my dehydrator?* Of course. You have a little more wiggle room for "too done" vs. "just right" at lower temps. It takes 12-24 hours, generally, to dehydrate fruit rolls. I definitely prefer the dehydrator because (a) I don't have to watch it, (b) it doesn't tie up the oven, (c) raw food retains more nutrients, and (d) I can fit a lot more in there, so I dirty the food processor or pots fewer times with greater yield.

✔ *What other fruits can I use?* I do a lot of strawberry rolls, and I hear peach/raspberry is delicious. The sky's the limit! Perhaps even mix fruit puree with plain yogurt for a probiotic and protein-boosted treat.

Healthy Upgrades: :

Try fermenting the fruit first! To 5 c. pureed fruit, add ½ tsp. salt, ¼ c. sweetener, and ¼ c. yogurt whey. Ferment at room temp 2 days until bubbly, then strain out the liquid with a tea towel or cheesecloth and proceed with dehydrating. *Note: Don't bother with fermenting if the rolls will get over 150F in the oven. More on fermenting here: http://bit.ly/jnq95V*

If you do have a dehydrator or access to one, you may enjoy making your own dried fruit. It's become one of our family's go-to snacks, since it's frugal, easy to eat, and can stay in the car or a purse for a really long time.

We regularly dehydrate apples and strawberries in season (I make strawberries into rolls because it's easier to blend than slice), and my husband likes to keep bananas at work.

Bonus: Homemade Cinnamon Applesauce

Work Intensity

Storage

Cost

We pick apples by the bushel in the fall, so making applesauce is the only way to use them all. It's also a great way to utilize bruised fruits and reduced price apples. Plus, the house smells wonderful.

Apples + Water + Cinnamon = Applesauce

Method:

You can peel the apples for easier digestion or leave the peels on for more fiber. Either way, wash, cut into quarters and take the core out.

Place into a pot with about ¼ c. water (sometimes less!) per 4-6 apples.

This won't look like enough, but it will be – there's a lot of water in an apple.

Add cinnamon to taste. I like a lot, so I usually just dump it on until I can hardly see the apples. You might start with ½ tsp. per 4 apples. You can always add cinnamon later, but you can't take it out.

Bring to a boil and cook on low, covered, until the apples are soft. Once they're falling apart you can either just stir well (without skins) for chunky applesauce or use a potato masher or hand blender for creamier applesauce.

If you left the skins on, or if your children don't do chunks, you'll need to blend or food process until smooth. I like to use an immersion blender so I'm not pouring hot sauce back and forth anywhere. With skins, blend a little longer than you think you'll need.

If your family is used to sweetened applesauce, you can add sugar when the sauce is warm. Start with 1/8 c. per 4 apples and see how little you can get away with. I prefer zero! Certain apples will make sweeter sauce, many say combining many varieties makes it sweeter, and cinnamon helps the illusion of sweetness as well.

Store cold for a long time, at least a month or more. Put into single servings right away to help speed up lunch packing. You can also freeze or can applesauce. Be sure to use proper canning times and techniques; see http://bit.ly/RzMXlJ for info.

Peanut Butter Kisses

Work Intensity

Storage

Cost

The staple snack on our counter in my childhood was peanut butter kisses: corn syrup, Jif peanut butter, powdered sugar and nonfat dried milk with mini chocolate chips. Not exactly real food, but oh, so addicting. When I discovered a healthier adaptation, I couldn't call my mom quickly enough to share!

Ingredients:

1 part natural peanut butter
1 part honey, raw if possible
1-2 parts unsweetened coconut
Other add-in options: mini chocolate chips, sesame seeds, flax meal, chopped crispy nuts or sunflower seeds

Method:

If there was an easier than easy icon, this recipe would get it. Just grab a bowl and fork, mix honey and peanut butter until uniform, then add the coconut until everything holds together like a sticky playdough. Grab a hunk, roll into a ball between your palms, and eat!

Add one or more of the optional add-ins before rolling if you like.

Store in an airtight container at room temperature, or wrap in waxed paper like a hard candy (twist both ends of a square/rectangular piece to make the wrapper) to serve them individually.

If you really need a recipe, use 1/3 cup peanut butter, 1/3 cup honey, and 2/3 cup coconut and you'll be just fine.

Note: Good substitutes for the coconut include flax meal or sesame seeds.

Makes as much as you choose to make!

 Added Bonus: Perfect for making with little ones, because there's no stress in measuring ingredients, and it's really fun to roll them into balls!

Thanks to Titus 2 Homemaker for giving me the idea!

Kid-Friendly Beef Jerky

Work Intensity

Storage

Cost

Dried meat products are so expensive to purchase, even when the meat is not well-sourced, but it's such a great way to have a packable, shelf-stable protein source. You'll be shocked at how easy this recipe is, especially if you don't have a dehydrator.

Ingredients

3 pounds ground beef
2 tsp. salt
¼-2 tsp. pepper
2 tsp. garlic powder or 4-8 cloves fresh garlic
2 ½ tsp. ground cumin
pinch cayenne (or just sprinkle it on top for super spicy!)

Method

In a small bowl, combine spices. In a larger bowl, use your hands or a potato masher to incorporate the dry spices into the meat. Press about 1/8" thick, as evenly as possible, onto parchment paper, silicone mats, or your dehydrator sheets. Use a butter knife to cut into strips of desired size (or put on your Excalibur dehydrator trays with parchment paper but without the mesh, which will create diamond-shaped pieces of jerky just with the weight of the meat, which you can then break apart).

In a dehydrator: Dehydrate at the highest temp (usually 150F) for 12-18 hours, flipping over after 6-8 hours.

In the oven: Set the oven to 200F. "Bake" the meat to dry it out for about 4 hours, flipping after each hour and pouring any grease off the tray/paper/mat.

When is it done? The jerky is done when there is no pink inside. Let a piece cool and then break it and squeeze – if you don't see any moisture leaking out, you're golden. Once cooled, the jerky will be considerably harder to break off and chew than when it first came out, so don't shoot too high.

Food safety: The USDA has something to say about jerky: The meat should be brought to an internal temp of 160F *before* dehydrating. Many recipes just say to dehydrate. Since I prefer the texture with the oven method, I'll mainly stick to that one and not worry. If you dehydrate, you can always bake the meat quickly first or even, apparently, steam it.

Storage: Store in an airtight bag or container. When at home, I like to store in the fridge just to prolong the life of my jerky and "be safe" from mold forming. It can last at room temperature for a really long time (months) when truly properly dried, though.

 Added Bonus: You can add dried fruit to make a more traditional "pemmican."

 FAQs

- ✓ *Why such a range on some of those spices?* Because while our family likes it spicy, others may not, so the lower range is what still has good flavor but no tongue tingling.
- ✓ *What's kid-friendly about this?* Ever watched a kid trying to eat real beef jerky? When made from a cut of meat, it's far too tough for their little jaws. The ground meat makes it easy to bite and chew.
- ✓ *Why is jerky both inexpensive and expensive?* The first time I tried my own beef jerky, I walked into my trusty butcher's shop and asked what meat he recommended for the job. I walked out cradling a small chunk of meat, eyes wide and wallet $20 lighter. !! The jerky was okay, but pretty tough. I'm happy to use the less expensive ground meat! Therefore, compared to buying high quality cuts of meat or purchasing jerky in a store, making your own is frugal. Compared to the actual cost of many other snacks, though, jerky is more expensive (but also more nutrient dense).
- ✓ *Did you say "mold" up there?* Yes. My first batch ever had some moisture in it somehow, and after a few weeks on the counter, it started growing mold. I left a small piece of my next batch in a baggie in the drawer as a test, and it was there for *months* without incident, so it's really all about how much moisture you can dehydrate out. (Both were dehydrated without using the oven.)
- ✓ *Can I use other meats?* I've only done beef. I added ground liver once, just a bit, but it really changed the flavor, so proceed with caution on that front. I'm sure other ground meats would also dehydrate well, but do follow food safety rules.

Used with permission from GNOWFGLINS.

Creamy Garlic Veggie Dip

Work Intensity

Storage

Cost

Never underestimate the appeal of a tasty dip with vegetables. When served before dinner to hungry families, veggies can go fast! This one helps you avoid the industrial oils common in processed dips and is super frugal.

Ingredients:

SF GF 🚫SW 🚫 🚫 🚫

- ½ c. yogurt cheese
- 2 minced garlic cloves
- 1 tsp. dried, minced chives OR ½ tsp dried cilantro
- 1 tsp. dried dill weed
- 3-4 grinds of fresh black pepper
- ¼ c. plain whole milk yogurt or sour cream
- ¼ tsp. salt
- 1 ½ tsp. lemon juice
- ½ tsp. onion powder

Method:

Mix all ingredients together thoroughly. Best chilled before serving for about an hour, but it works if you have to prepare the dip in a pinch to serve immediately. Adjust seasoning as needed. Perfect veggie dip for any crudite platter.

Makes the equivalent of a small tub of dip; double for a large party.

 Added Bonus: Fresh garlic fights sick bugs, too! And vampires. And kisses.

FAQs

- ✔ *Can I make the dip with fresh herbs?* It would be delicious. Just increase the quantities by 2-3x for fresh.
- ✔ *Can I make yogurt cheese with store yogurt?* The directions are exactly the same. You could also substitute cream cheese for yogurt cheese. (How to make yogurt cheese at http://bit.ly/ZFeIvb.)

Adapted from Shannon at Nourishing Days.

Katie's Mustard Potato Salad

Work Intensity

Storage

Cost

What's a good substitute for the munchy, crunchy snacks that come in individual packages like potato chips and pretzels? Potato salad may not be great for the car, but for school lunches it's one of my personal favorites. I've been known to eat it for breakfast!

Ingredients:

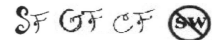

Potatoes
Eggs
Dill Pickles
Mayonnaise
Mustard
Salt and Pepper

Method:

There are countless takes on potato salad out there; mine is heavy on the mustard and dill pickles, and after the first time, you won't need this recipe again. Use equal numbers of potatoes, eggs, and pickle spears (fewer pickles if they're whole). For a family of four, I use four of each.

1. **Cook potatoes**: You can bake them with the skins on for about an hour at 400 degrees F, or peel, cut into cubes, and boil about 15 minutes until just tender. Watch them so you don't end up with mashed potato salad!
2. **Boil eggs**: Cover eggs with cold water and some salt, which prevents the egg from leaking out if one cracks. Bring to a boil, then turn off the heat, cover, and leave for 15 minutes to cook. Pour off the hot water and soak in cold water, switching the water a few times until cooled. If you're making the potato salad right away, you can crack the cooled eggs, return to the pot and allow them to sit a minute in the water, and then the shells will come off more easily.
3. **Dice both the potatoes and the eggs** into bite-sized pieces. You can choose to leave the skins on or off, regardless of how you cook the potatoes.
4. **Dice the pickles** into 1/8" squares.

In an appropriately sized bowl – give yourself some head room for stirring – mix potatoes, pickles, and eggs together with mayo and mustard. I eye it up: usually a Tablespoon-sized dollop or so of mayo per potato and a generous teaspoon-sized dollop of mustard per potato. Shoot low, because you can always add more, but you can't take it out! Salt and pepper to taste.

Makes any amount you'd like!

Timesaver: Bake potatoes with dinner or alongside Homemade Granola (p. 10) to save oven energy. Make extra hard-boiled eggs for easy snacks and lunches throughout the week.

 Added Bonus: Potato Salad goes great with hamburgers on the grill, and it can be made in advance for a get together. It's my favorite frugal dish to pass. Good for breakfast, lunch or dinner!

If you peel your potatoes, be sure to make Tater Skin Crispies (p. 52) for a truly portable, munchy snack!

Eggshells are great for the garden and compost piles.

I like getting the kids to help on this one. As young as two years old, kids can cut cooked potatoes with a butter knife and help peel hard-boiled eggs.

Healthy Upgrades & Variations:

- ✔ There aren't many commercially produced mayonnaise products that use real, traditional fats. Make your own with this simple method: http://bit.ly/cqNGkb.
- ✔ Leaving the skins on the potatoes adds extra iron. Baking the potatoes is the healthiest way to preserve nutrients, but some don't like the flavor baking imparts to potato salad.
- ✔ Try to find a source for eggs that allow their chickens to run around outside, organic if possible.
- ✔ Fresh eggs are notoriously hard to peel when hard-boiled. I am deeply in love with this trick from one of my favorite mothers of a brood: http://bit.ly/Tsn2e7
- ✔ Any pickles are delicious, but lacto-fermented pickles add probiotics to aid digestion.
- ✔ This dish can be very nourishing with homemade mayo; if you have to use processed mayo or Miracle Whip, the soybean oil involved is not good for you. If you use purchased stuff anyway, at the very least avoid the "light" versions, because they often use artificial sweeteners.
- ✔ If you worry about fat, go high on the mustard and lower on the mayo.
- ✔ Add a dash of pickle juice for extra zing. You can also substitute a bit of plain yogurt for the mayo, which will again add probiotics to your dish.
- ✔ Some people also like to add raw, chopped onions or celery.
- ✔ Adding fresh or dried dill or other herbs makes for an even fancier potato salad experience.

Cold Balsamic-n-Spelt Salad

Work Intensity

Storage

Cost

Pasta salads are practically a staple for a summer picnic gathering, and I've even seen them as "healthy" choices on school lunch menus. This unique dish takes advantage of the flexibility and versatility of pasta salad but uses proper whole grains and lots of in-season veggies.

Ingredients:

Cooked spelt (start with about 1 c. dry spelt berries)
Carrots
Pea pods   Red onion
Cubed cheese   Chopped broccoli
Green olives   Garbanzo beans (chickpeas)

Balsamic Vinaigrette Dressing:
1 Tbs. Dijon mustard
2 Tbs. balsamic vinegar   ½ tsp. thyme or Italian seasoning
½ c. Extra virgin olive oil   1 clove garlic, crushed

Method:

Cook the spelt berries according to package directions. Whole grain berries cook much like rice, usually one cup grain to two cups water. Bring to a boil and cook, covered, for about 45 minutes. Once the grains are chewy, drain any excess water. Chill the cooked grains.

To make dressing:
Whisk mustard and vinegar together. Slowly stream in the olive oil while whisking briskly. Stir in the other ingredients. Store any leftovers in a glass container, either at room temperature for a month or cold for longer The olive oil will firm up in the fridge, so give it an hour to liquefy before serving a tossed salad.

Chop veggies into bite-sized pieces Toss in a large bowl with cold grains and salad dressing to taste This salad is best if it's had at least an hour chilled to let the flavors meld together. You may want to add extra dressing when serving, especially if it's a day later.

Makes about 6-8 servings

Timesaver: Cook the grains the day before you need the salad while you're in the kitchen for dinner anyway.

 Added Bonus: This salad lasts well for a time out of the fridge, good for lunch packing purposes. The beans and whole grain are complimentary proteins.

Healthy Upgrades:

 Soaked option: Simply soak the spelt berries overnight at room temperature with warm water and a Tbs. of vinegar, then drain and cook as directed.

FAQs

✔ *Why the raw food icon?* Since the veggies and dressing impart awesome enzymes and raw vitamins to the dish, it seems worthy of "partially raw" at least.

✔ *Why soak the grains overnight?* See the Soaking Grains Primer on p. 82.

✔ *What does cooked spelt taste like?* When my husband and I first tasted the cooked spelt berries, we didn't have high hopes for the finished product. They're rather chewy, but once the flavors all got together, the chewiness was a surprisingly refreshing texture for a summer side dish.

✔ *Can I use other grains?* Certainly! Many people like quinoa, bulgur, and even millet in cold grain salads. Use your imagination and your pantry stock.

✔ *Can I add meat?* To make a main dish cold salad, meat is a great addition.

✔ *Can I use other veggies?* That's the beauty of cold grain salads. Like pasta salads, they're incredibly versatile based on what you have on hand and your personal tastes. For this version, I think the red onion really makes the dish, but everything is ultimately optional. Some people like raisins, nuts, and even cooked veggies like sweet potato, beets or turnips. Here are some other variations that I use for pasta salad:

Greek Salad
Garbanzo beans, baby spinach leaves, feta cheese, cherry tomatoes, red onion, Greek dressing, optional: olives (green or black)

Red Pepper Italian
1 red pepper, Pepper Jack cheese, broccoli, cherry tomatoes, red onion slices, crushed red pepper to taste, Homemade Italian dressing with added Parmesan cheese, optional: jalapeno or banana peppers

Cold Pizza Salad
Green pepper, pepperoni, mozzarella cheese, green olives, chopped tomatoes, broccoli, Sun-dried tomato dressing or Homemade Italian with sun-dried tomatoes

Stovetop Cinnamon Rice Pudding

Work Intensity   Storage   Cost

Homemade stovetop rice pudding, not to be confused with baked rice pudding, has got to be my favorite dessert – mostly because I can still get away with eating it for breakfast, unlike ice cream!

Ingredients:

1 c. brown rice	1 tsp. vanilla
2 c. boiling water	¾ c. sugar OR sucanat
4 c. milk	1 Tbs. (or more) butter

SF GF 🚫 S

Method:

Boil the rice in water for 10 minutes. Drain off the water carefully (don't use a large-holed colander).

Add milk and bring carefully to a boil over medium to medium-low heat, with the cover off, stirring often. Be sure to scrape the bottom of the pan as milk can burn easily.

Once you reach a boil, turn the burner to low, cover, and cook 45-90 minutes until pudding is thick and milk seems to have all been absorbed. Don't stir too often during this time, but watch for scorching on the bottom of the pan.

When thickened, remove the pan from heat; then add sweetener, vanilla and butter and stir. Serve warm or cold with cinnamon.

Makes 8 servings

 Timesaver: A double batch works great with rice pudding.

 Added Bonus: Milk and whole grains make a complete protein, so this dessert is definitely vying for a slot in the "health foods" category at your house.

Healthy Upgrades:

S **Soaked option:** You can soak the rice overnight at room temperature using either a germinated brown rice method or accelerated fermentation. (http://bit.ly/hACQf9)

Get more soaked grain recipes with a FREE 85-page ebook online under eBooks heading at http://www.KitchenStewardship.com

No White Sugar option: Substitute 1/3-½ cup honey to taste for the white sugar. If using raw honey, wait until the finished rice pudding is cool enough that it doesn't hurt your finger. This will preserve the enzymes. You could certainly use maple syrup as well, but that's usually twice as expensive. (If you wish to use maple syrup, try almond flavoring in place of the vanilla for a special treat!)

Less sweetener: I've cut the sweetener already by a quarter from the full cup in the original recipe, but going down to ½ cup total is still pretty tasty.

FAQs

✔ *How do I know when it's done?* It takes longer than I expect every time to get all that milk absorbed. Just be patient – the pudding is done when there's no more liquid milk swimming around and it has a tapioca pudding kind of consistency. It will also thicken up in the refrigerator, if it makes it to storage before being eaten.

✔ *How do I serve it?* Cold or warm, add cinnamon to taste. Raisins make it a special treat.

✔ *Want a real indulgence?* The original recipe calls for white rice and tastes even better (less chewy). Just follow the same directions except you only boil the rice in water 3 minutes and cook for 15-45 minutes until done.

Chocomole (Pudding)

Work Intensity

Storage

Cost

This goodie has one of those ingredients lists that you might want to keep under wraps until after the family tries and enjoys the "pudding." It still amazes me that it works so well!

Ingredients

1 medium sized avocado
¼ c. honey
¼ c. cocoa powder
1 tsp. vanilla

Method

Scoop the avocado out of its shell and place all the ingredients in a blender or food processor. Puree well. Serve cold when possible; best within the first 12 hours.

Pit trick: To get the avocado pit out cleanly, whack it with a big old knife, right in the center. Rotate the knife like the hands of a clock, and the pit will usually pop right out.

Makes about 4 small servings.

 Added Bonus: A great dairy-free, nut-free, grain-free dessert or snack for those with food allergies!

Variations

Banana-mole: Toss one very ripe banana into the mix. I recommend starting with half and tasting.

Coco-Choco: Add ¼ c. shredded coconut to the mix (but you have to be okay   with chunky pudding). Try adding a few Tbs. unrefined coconut oil for something different without chunks.

FAQs

- ✓ *Will I taste the avocado?* Ideally, not at all. If you do, add a bit more cocoa, honey, or both. If you don't know it's in there, you really would never guess.
- ✓ *How do I get avocados frugally?* I always buy 3-4 avocados when they're on sale – you can leave one on the counter to ripen up and store the others in the fridge immediately. Take them out one at a time to ripen, and you'll have fresh avocado for this recipe, guacamole, or to put on top of salads for 10-14 days. Maybe buy 5 or 6 when they're on sale...
- ✓ *How do I know when an avocado is ripe?* Similar to a pear, pinch on the top gently, and if there's really any give at all, it's probably ripe. An overripe avocado is quite yucky, for lack of a better word. Unfortunately, once you cut into an under-ripe avocado, it's too late to do much about it, and they're not all that great either.
- ✓ *What if my avocado is ready before I am?* Put it in the fridge immediately! If you have an avocado on the counter ripening up and you'd rather wait a day or two to use it once you notice the tell-tale softness, get it right into the fridge. Typically it will wait for you for a few days.
- ✓ *How long can I store chocomole?* Not long, unfortunately. Avocados show their age quickly, and the pudding will taste "off" within a day or two.

Recipe adapted from Ciao-Chow (http://bit.lyUat2g1)

Easy Vanilla Pudding

Work Intensity   **Storage**   **Cost**

Pudding cups are often seen as a snack, but they're really a dessert. This might be a dessert, too, but at least it's better for you!

Ingredients

½ c. sugar or sucanat
4 ½ Tbs. cornstarch OR 3-4 Tbs. arrowroot starch
¼ tsp. salt
3 c. whole milk
2 tsp. vanilla
1 Tbs. butter

Method

In a heavy-bottomed, medium-sized saucepan, whisk sugar, starch and salt. Pour milk in slowly while whisking.

Heat over medium or medium-low, whisking occasionally, until bubbles form on the edges or top. The mixture will begin to thicken and coat the back of a spoon or hang onto the whisk. Do not allow a full boil.

Cook and stir constantly for 2 minutes after the bubbly/coated point. Remove from heat and stir in butter and vanilla.

Pour into one large serving bowl or individual glass bowls. Chill at least 2 hours before serving.

Serves 6.

Smoothies & Other Yogurt Variations

I don't do sauerkraut, fermented pickles, or kefir, so yogurt is my main source of probiotics. That's so important to me that I eat it at least once a day, and my family goes through at least a gallon a week! There are lots of ways to eat yogurt beyond "with a spoon". Here are some of our favorites:

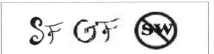

- ✔ Green smoothies
- ✔ With cinnamon applesauce
- ✔ With honey on the spoon
- ✔ With frozen fruit
- ✔ Yogurt cheese and jelly/honey sandwiches

Ingredients:

Green Smoothies:

    Kale, Spinach or Dark Leaf Lettuce
    1 c. milk
    ½-1 c. plain yogurt
    1 frozen banana
    A few handfuls frozen fruit: strawberries, blueberries, peaches, etc.
    Other boosters: kelp powder, coconut oil, flax seed, natural peanut butter

Makes 3-4 servings, depending on the age of your kids.

Method:

Put the greens in the blender container and blend with only the milk and yogurt for a few minutes until the greens are totally obliterated. Add fruit and blend until incorporated.

 Timesaver: Use the blender for making bread crumbs from stale heels first, then rinse and make a smoothie. I love to save on dishes!

Another tip is to put all your smoothie ingredients – frozen fruit, cubes of whey, powder supplements, etc. – in a grocery bag in the freezer. Pull it out and whip up a fast smoothie!

Healthy Upgrades:

When including coconut oil, it's imperative to do it correctly or you'll end up with little beads of hard oil in the smoothie that are quite unpalatable. You must melt the oil first, then stream in through the top of the blender directly into the vortex. If the oil gets mixed in thoroughly before the cold smoothie has a chance to harden it, it will stay mixed. If not, your husband might not let you make smoothies anymore without suspicion.

FAQs

✔ *Can smoothies last for storing/traveling?* If you make the smoothie right before leaving, it's great for travel (in the right kind of cup, of course). My kids don't mind it when it's a day old, but I don't think it's very tasty. If we have extras, I freeze in single servings and put in lunchboxes. Frozen smoothie thaws just right by lunchtime.

✔ *How do I decide how much yogurt to add?* The yogurt will make the smoothie more tart, so your family's tastes dictate that one.

✔ *Can I sweeten it up if I don't like the result?* Absolutely. First, I think frozen, slightly overripe bananas go a looooong way in making a smoothie seem sweeter. I peel brown bananas, break them in half and throw them in a zippered bag in the freezer just for smoothies. Alternately, you can always add a squeeze of raw honey, and the coconut oil will give it a fighting chance against sugar-loving families, too.

✔ *I read that I'm supposed to cook spinach and kale first to avoid oxalic acid. How do I do that with a smoothie?* I do lightly steam my greens first, then freeze them in ice cube trays or just very flat in a bag. Break it apart by banging on the counter. Three cubes of greens is about right for my family's smoothie size. You can also use freshly cooked greens in a smoothie, as everything else is cold enough to compensate. Raw spinach and kale shouldn't cause problems unless you eat them every day.

✔ *Cinnamon applesauce with yogurt?* It's refreshingly different, and my favorite way to enjoy yogurt with zero sweetener.

✔ *Honey on the spoon?* If you put honey right on your spoon, you can get just a smidge with each bite and ultimately get more sweetness and less sweetener.

✔ *How do I find yogurt cheese?* You make it. The tutorial is linked here online http://bit.ly/ZFelvb. It looks, acts, and tastes more or less like cream cheese. My son adores yogurt cheese, sliced strawberries and honey on whole wheat bread. Save a bit for Creamy Garlic Veggie Dip (p. 70).

✔ *Isn't yogurt kind of expensive?* No way! I make my own. At the very least, buy the big tubs of plain yogurt and add your own fruit. If you get brave, try making homemade yogurt. I promise: it's easy, quick, and can save hundreds of dollars a year.

✔ Recipes for making and using homemade yogurt are available on Kitchen Stewardship's "Healthy Snacks to Go" print edition bonus content page at: http://bit.ly/ZFelvb

What Does it Mean to Soak Grains?

Because grains and nuts are seeds by their nature, they are designed to propagate a species, not necessarily to be food for humans. They are stocked with anti-nutrients that inhibit digestion, bind nutrients, and make the seed less likely to be eaten, or at least more likely to be passed through. Many animals have systems that can combat the anti-nutrients in seeds; human beings need to fight them in the kitchen.

Throughout this book, when you see the symbol:

It means there is a soaked grain (or nut) option for the recipe. Sometimes soaking is very little or no extra work, but other times it's a lot of work. You'll have to decide for yourself if it's worth it. Some people can simply tell they don't digest grains well and have found that with these processes, they feel better. Others trust the science that says that soaking increases mineral and nutrient absorption for better overall health .

Method:

Soaking grains is both a mild fermentation process and a mimicking of the germination or sprouting process. It is not necessary with white flour or processed grains, but only when the bran is included. Find the science behind the process, some various theories and more recipes here: http://bit.ly/SIFfJ6. Basically, you need to soak your whole grains or flour:

✔   in a slightly acidic medium
✔   in liquid, preferably above body temperature
✔   or 12-24 hours
✔   at or above room temperature
✔   with some wheat or spelt involved

1. To obtain the proper pH, add at least 1 Tbs. of vinegar (any kind), yogurt, buttermilk, lemon juice, whey, or sourdough starter per cup of water. You can also soak completely in yogurt or buttermilk if the recipe calls for a milk product.
2. For optimal results, heat water in a teapot until it is just uncomfortable to the touch, but not boiling, about 120-140 degrees F.
3. Most people simply start their recipes "soaking" the night before they're going to prepare the food by preparing the entire recipe and letting it sit on the counter.
4. Do not refrigerate the grains. Store in the warmest place in your kitchen for best results, such as the top of the refrigerator, on the stovetop, especially if you use the oven for dinner, or even in the oven with the light on.
5. Phytase is the enzyme responsible for breaking down the major anti-nutrients, phytates and phytic acid. It is only found in sufficient quantities in wheat, spelt and buckwheat, so if a recipe uses only oats , you'll notice a few Tablespoons of wheat flour added in the soaking instructions.

Reduced Waste Healthy Lunch Packing

Eating on the go can sometimes be unhealthy not only for your body, but for the earth. When you're making food from scratch, an added bonus is that you are in charge of the packaging. You can save money *and* the earth by checking out these lunch packing tips to
Reduce Waste   ⭘   Increase Nutrition   ⭘   Simplify your Time

1. Reuse plastic baggies. When something is dry, especially if you are going to pack the same thing, like crackers, a few days in a row, ask your children to bring home their empty baggies and refill them for the next day's lunch. This saves time and money, too!

2. Use glass storage containers over plastic when possible. Glass is easier to wash in the dishwasher and doesn't leach any harmful chemicals. You can also seek out stainless steel containers, which are lighter weight than glass.

3. Avoid single serving drinks. Use a water bottle like the Klean Kanteen stainless steel water bottles or a reusable glass bottle (like from Snapple).

4. Avoid baggies altogether. Use cloth bags, stainless steel or even plastic containers for sandwiches and fruits/vegetables. Chances are you can reuse twice to avoid dishes.

5. Timesaver: package in single-serving sizes right away. When you're making something like granola bars or power bars, put some bars into baggies or wrap in waxed paper to store individually. You've got your own convenience foods ready to go!

6. Some purchased foods are good for lunches: Natural applesauce single cups, or better yet, jarred applesauce in your own cups; pita bread and hummus; string or pre-sliced cheese, baby carrots, whole fruits.

7. **Institute this rule: *"Whatever goes to school, comes home, unless you have eaten it."*** This accomplishes two things: you reduce waste because you can reuse bags and leftover food, AND you know what your kids eat and don't eat. That helps you (hopefully together with the kids) pack better lunches in the future.

8. **Use an assembly line.** Line up the lunchboxes, line up the supplies, and work with a plan. Keeping your assembly space organized goes a long way.

9. **Pack a napkin!** Cloth, if you want to save the earth, but any old napkin will do so that your kid isn't the one saying, "I need a napkin!" That drove me nuts as a teacher, and now I always forget to include napkins, in a cruel twist of ironic fate.

10. **Involve the kiddos.** Kids should have a hand in both the packing and unpacking/putting away processes. Try making a list of various acceptable lunch foods in categories like *main course, fruit, veggie, snack*. Your child(ren) can choose one from each category and help you pack it. See more lunch packing tips at KitchenStewardship.com.

About Katie Kimball:

I'm Katie Kimball, a Catholic wife and mother of three who wants the best of nutrition and living for her family. My educational background is actually in elementary education and English, but as I began cooking for my children and reading about nutrition, I quickly became a home chef and researcher. In early 2009 I began my journey as an online writer, and I'm head over heels in love with the tangled web that is the blogging career.

I believe that God calls us to be good stewards of all His gifts as we work to feed our families: time, finances, the good green earth, and of course, our healthy bodies. KitchenStewardship.com seeks to share with others ways to balance all four and be prayerful in the call to vocation in the kitchen.

I'm far from perfect: my kitchen is often a mess, I lose my patience with family members, and I certainly spend too much time on the computer. But I do my best to provide optimal nutrition and health for my loved ones, which means I spend a lot of time in the kitchen. I make everything from scratch and talk about food all the time. I also strive to make things taste good, which is where you benefit. Thank you so much for your purchase of the second edition of *Healthy Snacks to Go*, and please let me know if there are any problems or if the text does not meet expectations (I'd provide a full refund).

Acknowledgments:

No writer or chef can stand alone. (Isn't eating snacks alone some sort of issue, anyway?) I'm deeply thankful for a network of other bloggers, writers, and eaters who helped the original book become a reality. Opinionators and editors include:
Sarah of *Heartland Renaissance*, Lenetta of *Nettacow*, Jen of *Happy Little Homemaker*, Kate of *Modern Alternative Mama*, Jen of *A Heavenly Perspective*, Paula of *The Chicken Coop*, my faithful commenters Sonia, Emily and Sarah W and my mom, who has always been my best editor, even of my speech and thoughts.

Many thanks to the ladies at my son's Atrium program and my Bible study for taste testing power bars for me and giving opinions.

For the second edition, I'm grateful again to Lenetta Kuehn for editing, and also for the grammatical and editing skills of Erin Odom and Pam Farley. I invited many Facebook fans and Twitter followers to help test recipe remakes, and to them and their families, thank you so much!

SF   GF   CF   (SW)   (no grain)   (no nut)   (no raw)   [S]

Sugar Free | Gluten Free | Caesin Free | No Added | Grain Free | Nut Free | Raw Food | Soaked
Sweetener   Option